INTRODUCTION AND SUPPORTING PROJECTS

What began as a letter from a father to his children has resulted in this publication, which I hope others will find informative and useful in similar situations. The information contained herein is a personal account of one man's (mine) experience and process after being diagnosed with the potentially terminal illness of Parkinson's Plus disease with Multi Systems Atrophy (MSA). As a father of six adult children, a husband, friend and business associate, I will document, within my own experience, the impact this disease has had on my relationships with all encompassed in my life, as well as the financial aspects involved to ensure that all matters are put in order for the protection of self and loved ones. Within this context, I have attempted to add a dose of grassroots wisdom, common business sense, spiritual advice, technical and legal information, as well as financial processes. While obviously very serious in content, it is designed to be an easy-flowing and somewhat light-hearted account of what one might expect to experience in a similar situation, and it is intended to aide others in

avoiding some of the landmines that are lurking out there waiting to trip you up.

Accompanying this publication is a recommendation in the form of a plea to the President of the United States, as well as both presidential candidates to find a cure for Parkinson's and to please simplify the community that has grown to support the cause.

Since this publication is an autobiography, it will most probably be completed by someone else. It is this author's wish that the completion of this book will be penned by the historian of the U.S. Alliance Organization focused on the cure for Parkinson's.

PREFACE

This book assumes that you either have been diagnosed with or know someone that has been diagnosed with what is referred to as a chronic, life-threatening or terminal illness. This is an insider's perspective aimed at dealing with all issues that must be faced and addressed when you're hit with that reality. It will deal with the cold, hard facts without pulling punches. I will add levity where possible, because without it, the subject is far too depressing. Besides, if you can't laugh at yourself then who can you laugh at? It is also meant to be a lesson in life dedicated to my children. Life comes at us too fast sometimes, and there has been no exception to this rule in my family. Throughout my lifetime, the biggest regret I have is not making and taking enough time to teach my children some of the lessons in life the ways I now perceive I should have. Although this writing can never make up for those lost lessons, my hope is that it is a way to begin the healing. What I can promise you is that I always gave 150% of what I knew how to give, and when you move that quickly, you will make mistakes, learn from them, apologize when necessary and move on. Don't look back, and don't slow down. Use the new information you learned from previous mistakes to better make the next decision and understand that if this is a decision that will allow a 'do over,' you will be more successful going 95 out of 100 than one-for-one. Think about it - a baseball player makes the Hall of Fame if he hit .333.

One added thought - I began putting the ideas together for this book almost a year ago. Since then, we have had the privilege of hearing the advice of Randy Pausch on Dateline, as well as his sharing of his book titled *The Last Lecture*. I did see a good part of the dateline episode and a subsequent follow-up report on Oprah, but I have yet to read his book. I will read it the second I finish penning my thoughts for this book. My fear is that great minds think alike, and so I hope my information comes across as fresh and original. (Update: Randy passed away today, July 25, 2008. Our thoughts and prayers go out to his family. With sincere gratitude, we honor him for taking a leadership role and for the invaluable contributions he made in his lifetime.

THE COLLECTION

You have been named CEO of <insert your name hear> Inc. Make sure you company runs like a finely tuned machine

About the logic

Understand your mission statement

Developing your goal and objectives

 Know you limitations

Understanding your competition

Understanding your new Financial Statement

Understanding your sources of income

Understanding your expenses

Have a plan for when you are gone

Develop a planning horizon

Succession and progression planning

My timeline to date

TMI

Be Prepared!!!

Hire the Right People

Understanding you organization chart

Hiring and Firing authority

The interview process

Who are all these people?

Your Doctors

If 9 out of 10 doctors agree find the 10th and make sure you understand why!!!

Find a psychologist!

Introducing the CEO of Mark Bosche, Inc.

MARK EUGENE BOSCHE

Born March 10, 1959, in Cape Girardeau, Missouri to Jean C. and Gene R. Bosche - both third generation German immigrants.

They say that you can often describe a person by the titles they have had over the years. If this is true, then my list would read: Son, Godson, Catholic, Brother (x3), Cousin, Friend, Student, Altar Boy, Classmate, Teammate, Boyfriend, Camp Counselor, Assistant Forest Ranger, Junior Class President, Assistant Manager, Senior Class President, Graduate, Park Ranger, Teamster, College Student, Spartan, Fiancé, Father(x4), Husband, Neighbor, Brother-in-law, Operations Manager, Programmer, Account Manager, Coach, Board Member, Farmer, Village Trustee, Planning Commission Chairman, Mayor Pro-tem, Sales Director, Investor, Internet Company Founder, Corporate Vice President, Father-in-law, Divorcee, Grandfather (x6), Stepfather (x2) and most recently, which is why I am writing this book, Patient, Parkinson's victim, retired and disabled, by definition only, and now a support group member and wannabe author who is trying to avoid the new titles of bankrupt, insane and deceased.

There are many titles on the list above that I am very proud of and some that I am not so proud of, but one thing is for sure, they all have been learning experiences that have guided me through life. These personal, business, political, and most recently, medical experiences are the basis for many of the ideas expressed in this book. As you may have guessed, I have lived and continue to live a very blessed life and have a number of people to be grateful to for the love, friendship, education, guidance and inspiration that have

5

been afforded me over the years. This list is way too long to spell out here, but you know who you are. I can't often claim an original thought, but one thing I do consider myself good at is taking an idea, embellishing it and finding a good application for it. So to all the co-contributors to this book that have given me these many pearls of wisdom over the years, I graciously thank you. Special thanks goes to Dan Siadak, my oldest son's father-in-law and friend, for the concept of titles describing one's life, as Dan used a similar line of titles to begin his welcome speech during our children's wedding.

Most of all, I would like to thank my parents. I consider myself part of the Lucky Sperm Club - not because of the wealth and standing in the community they provided me, as we actually lived what many would consider to be very comfortable, middle class standards in the Midwest during my formative years, but because of the their union back in the summer of 1958 that produced the raw material (ME) that they embellished, put in motion and set in the right direction, which enabled the writing of this book and hopefully series of books entitled "My Way." A series of mostly autobiographical books aimed at various subject areas that defined my life. They will be told in a light-hearted and often comical way at times and aimed at a particular subject or phase in my life. They are meant to help my children understand from where they came and to provide historical documentation of our family history, and most importantly serve as a learning instrument in dealing with challenges in our everyday lives.

To my mother who provided the nurturing and love that gave me the confidence to do many of the things that defined the titles above, and who would not allow me to become complacent in my skills by constantly forcing me to explore new things in the fields of the arts, politics, religion and education. To my father, who provided me with the lessons in human nature, which in the writing of his Eulogy, I titled "Recipes for Life." Many of which helped shape this document, many of which I have combined and embellished to form the rules I live my life by. The one most appropriate rule for what you are about to read and the key to my sanity I believe is:

> *People are but a collection of idiosyncrasies that are defined by the laws of human nature. The better you understand the laws and how they have been applied in the development and embellishment of that individual, the better you will be able to understand and predict their behavior. Be respectful of their uniqueness and learn from them, for society, through the tools of business, politics, religion, science, gamesmanship and social norms, will continually try and mold them to commonality for reasons of economy and control, and if successful, would alter the definition of the human race. Your legacy will be judged by how well you can sort out the good qualities from the bad and how well you can utilize the resources that result.*

Mark Bosche - 2008

INTRODUCTION OF MY DISEASE

My intent here is not to create a definitive guide to dealing with Parkinson's or PSP, MSA or whatever they finally determine ails me, but rather, to share my life experiences in the hopes that it makes the road a little easier for someone else who has the patience to read this story. I will tell you that if you are looking for a scientific methodology or explanation of Parkinson's, you are in the wrong place. Instead, what you will find is a collection of ideas, informational sources and resources that hopefully act as a guide through your journey as a patient or caregiver affected by Parkinson's. I believe that every life experience, whether good or bad, is a learning experience and failure to learn will only lead to making the same mistakes over again. Since I have definitely (made plenty of mistakes lol) had plenty of experiences in my life - some multiple times - I consider myself well-qualified and hope that by sharing my experiences, I can help expedite or smooth out someone else's journey, and that they may pass it on to someone else making the journey. I will try to keep this somewhat light-natured, because this stuff is serious enough as it is, so please don't mistake my levity for a lack of conviction to finding a cure no matter how small a piece of the story this might be.

My journey officially began on January 5, 2006. I use this date because if there were earlier symptoms, they were not severe enough or seen as relative until later. I awoke one morning with my left arm asleep. I figured I had slept on my arm, and it would again awake and everything would be normal. Well, it soon woke up, but there was a sense of rigidness and some loss of function. For a couple of days, there was no improvement. Instead, there was a growing sense of numbness and rigidness in the arm. I called my doctor and got in to see him that same day. After reviewing my vital signs, he started ruling out all of the obvious conditions such as stroke, heart conditions, etc. The thought quickly shifted to nerve damage with the idea that I had slept on the arm and deprived it of blood. Another symptom that appeared for the first time back in December 2005 was an abnormal blood sugar test, just barely above the diabetic 125 problem line. So I had a follow-up appointment with my endocrinologist. The blood sugar problem appeared to be back in line; however, my growth hormone levels were abnormally high. I was referred to another doctor for an EMG test on my arm that came back normal. I must admit, I was thoroughly confused by the string of events, and even scarier, so were my doctors.

During the following six weeks, my wife and I took a trip to London for the Christmas holiday, and then we spent two weeks in Las Vegas and Dallas. During this trip, a new symptom appeared. It was a general sense of weakness, as well as fatigue. Upon my return, it was back to the doctors for more tests. This time an MRI, more blood tests and new medications for the diabetic symptoms. Next, a referral to a neurosurgeon who suspected a tumor was forming and was looking to operate on something. Again, there was nothing. Finally, in May 2006, we started making progress. I was referred to Dr. Kersti Bruining and her staff in Traverse City, Michigan. After a brief examination, which included seeing me walk in the room, she informed me she suspected some version of Young Onset Parkinson's. An initial visit to Mayo Clinic in Rochester, Minnesota in August 2006 confirmed her suspicion.

It was then I heard the knock at the door from a stranger that I had no experience with - an unwanted visitor that would not only be with me every moment, but would also define the pace and direction for the rest of my life, regardless of my desire or actions to distance myself from him. One that would test my mental stability, my religious beliefs and the foundations of my families and friends. My parents always encouraged me to choose my friends wisely, and I felt I had done a pretty good job with that. My success in that regard would become more evident, as the next few months of my life played out. This story, if I have done my job correctly, will outline the steps, whether by choice, fate or coincidence, my circle of influence is taking to cull the unwelcome guest from my life. Whether there is a happy ending or not will probably not be penned by me, and only God knows how this story will end. But, I invite you to come along for the ride and would encourage you to participate if you feel the urge to be part of the solution.

There are many ways to help out. A good place to start is by contacting one of the many foundations popping up out there. The Michael J. Fox Foundation www.michaeljfox.org and The Mohammed Ali Parkinson Center www.maprc.com websites are great places to start. If this story follows my dreams www.parkinsonsMSAsupport.com, a multimedia support group dealing with the subjects in this book, will become a reality and an additional resource for those seeking information, support and ways to contribute, as we continue to search for a cure. As you read this book, you will find that the ideas, although created originally to deal with my MSA problem, are probably suitable processes for dealing with most diseases similar to or resulting in the same end point. This may be true, but given the lesson in competition you will read later in the book, I don't believe that it is the best use of Mark E. Bosche, Inc. Although, in the interest of the bigger race, I will be open to sharing so feel free to contact me.

If I really do my job, you will find us as part of a national coalition of organizations focused on finding the cure for Parkinson's. This organization will consist of the existing, but streamlined, Charity, Research, Government, Support Group, Medical and Educational entities focused on the cure for Parkinson's and hopefully, for my sake, MSA.

You have been named CEO of (insert your name here), Inc. Make sure your company runs like a finely-tuned machine. Your life depends on it!

Shortly after being diagnosed, I was talking to a good friend of mine named Mike T. In our conversation, Mike talked about a concept of running your life as if you were just named its CEO, and making your decisions on life and healthcare based on sound business practices. He said as you make these decisions, be sure your Mission Statement, goals and objectives have been factored into the equation. This conversation was the inspiration that I needed to get this work started. To me, it was such a simple concept to grasp that the words just started flowing. Mike also deserves some credit because he, like me, can take a story and embellish it enough to make it useful for the situation at hand. By the way, Mike is full of many different pearls of wisdom that may well be expressed throughout the book. I tried to get Mike to sit down and talk with me for additional subject matter, but he had to get back to running Mike T., Inc. I hope he writes his own book one day.

ABOUT THE LOGIC

Human nature dictates that there is no one more interested in your health and well being than you. Likewise, there is no one that that knows how you would like to live your life or not, spend your money or not, or what kind of legacy you leave behind than the person staring back at you when you look into the mirror. Now, if you were a board of directors looking for someone to run your company who would you put in charge? Wouldn't you look for someone who possessed the qualities defined above? Many of the people I have talked to about this logic immediately respond that they do not feel qualified, educated or organized enough to run a company, much less the next couple of years with all the complications being added to their life! To which I respond, "You have been doing it since you were born. You might need some higher education or to hone some skills or maybe develop a new life strategy, but guess what, there is no one out there that can or will fire you. You have the job for life." So pick yourself up by your boot straps and get to it, because your company is about to greatly increase its spending habits and its exposure to risks in ways you have never imagined possible, and the quicker you take control of the helm, the better chance you have of success. If there are areas that you feel particularly weak in then do what most CEO's do - surround yourself with good people, you are going to need them!

CREATING AND UNDERSTANDING YOUR MISSION STATEMENT

There have been millions of dollars and countless hours spent on analyzing why most small businesses fail to meet their potential, and I think I have been copied on most of them in my email. So let's save some of the precious time we all don't have, and let me boil them down for you. Most businesses fail because they lack a plan for success. The concept was either a bad one or mistimed, and they are under-funded and lack the people they need to do the job. Life is not much different with the exception of a couple of human factors added, such as genetics, or as I would jokingly refer to, the Lucky Sperm Club. For example, someone like Prince

Charles who was handed his position because of the family he was born into. Many people get to some point in their lives and wonder where it all went. You know the feeling - time, money, and friends can all disappear very quickly if not cared for. So now that you are thinking about it, for whatever reason, let's put a plan together. It's time to do some soul searching! Ask yourself some questions, and take notes!

How prepared are you for dealing with your situation from an emotional, financial and spiritual perspective? "Let's have a moment of silence." We have all heard it at one time in our lives. You know, you bow your head and say a prayer for the deceased, and reminisce about the kind of person they were. We think thoughts like what a good friend, father and businessman, or hopefully not "Man, was he ever a bum!" Now, let's change the game a little and make the moment of silence for you. How do you want to be remembered and by whom? In other words, what is your legacy? Chances are that if you are reading this book, many of those opinions are already formed, but this may be your last chance to help define your legacy and accentuate the messages you always wanted to pass on to your kids - not for selfish reasons, but because you consider it worth learning.

Ask yourself the following questions:

> ➢ How prepared mentally are you for what is ahead of you?

> ➢ Are you at peace with yourself, your spouse, your God, your Kids?

> ➢ What loose ends do you need to tie up?

> ➤ Do you want to define the end, or do you want it done for you?

> ➤ What steps can you take to find a cure - if not for yourself, then for others, and how far are you willing to go?

> ➤ Who are you going to depend on, and what do you need to do to make sure they are ready and willing to help? To what level can you make their job easier, since you are about to ask them a huge favor?

> ➤ Are you becoming obsessed with your demise, and if so, what are you going to do to create a diversion for you, your friends and your family?

Now, I would encourage you to *stop reading at this point, put the book down, think about these questions and make some notes*. If you're back to reading in five minutes, you haven't spent enough time pondering the questions nor have you taken enough notes, so repeat the above process again and again. I think I spent months on these questions before I finally realized I was experiencing analysis paralysis, but you get my point. These answers will define your Mission Statement, Goals and Objectives. Okay, now you're probably starting to think this sounds like a lot of work, and that you'd rather meet your demise suddenly and quickly. If that thought just crossed your mind, step back and rethink question number one, because whether you agree yet or not, you have been given a gift. The bad news is you possibly have a terminal illness. The good news is God has decided to give you the time to get your affairs in order and do it right. Since I started working on this book, I have talked to a lot of people about the various concepts and topics I would be including throughout, and to this day, it continues to surprise me how many people have not lifted a finger to take any action toward putting their own plan and safeguards in place. I attribute this to simple human nature and our tendency to procrastinate, as well as our fear of death and dealing with the realities of death. We consider ourselves bulletproof or other matters continue to take priority. I urge you to choose one thing, such as making out your will, and focus on completing that task. Take a break after you complete your chosen task, if you need to, and then choose another task. Choose *one* – it doesn't matter which one. Then, step back and close your eyes and imagine the world without you in it tomorrow. Does the picture in your mind involve a probate court judge deciding the fate of your fortune with an unknown lawyer working with your grieving wife and kids? If so, you know what your number one priority is, so let's get moving!

At the end of this exercise you might end up with a *Mission Statement* that reads something like this:

Through the efforts of my personal health and well being corporation, I vow to find ways to improve my longevity and quality of life for both myself and my family while preserving and setting up a working estate plan that allows my family to live comfortably and minimizes the impact of the change in my health position. Further, I will strive to leverage my new position as a Young Onset Parkinson patient to help others find ways to deal with this disease in any way possible, including improved education, research, medicinal routines, financial planning or development of a cure.

DEVELOPING YOUR GOALS AND OBJECTIVES

This is an exercise we have probably all done in one way or another. Let's make sure the end results achieve the following:

➢ Make sure your goals are prioritized in order of importance, as you may have less time than you think.

➢ Do you have a goal to solve all of the issues identified in the soul searching exercise?

➢ Did you address all your key stake holders?

➢ Can the goals be achieved in short, definable periods?

➢ Are they in line with your final instructions on file?

When your goal exercise is done, you may end up with something like this:

➢ Develop a patient (meaning you) centric care plan including caregivers, facilities, doctors, insurance plans and medical supply needs. Define financial constraints and limitations of this plan within defined planning horizons.

➢ Develop financial and final instruction documents including wills, living trusts, insurance instruments and income and expense budgets.

➢ Develop a working cure plan leaving it nimble enough to readily change direction in the event of new developments in science, technology and patient care techniques.

➢ Become a valued and contributing member of the YOPD community as a patient, leader, educator or medical research contributor.

➢ Develop and execute a religious/spiritual rejuvenation plan.

> ➤ Do not become obsessed with your demise, and create a diversion plan for you and your family and friends.

Once your goals have been defined, it is time to assign specific objectives to each and begin executing. Using my own goals as an example, it will look something like this:

- ➤ Wills
- ➤ Living trusts
- ➤ Insurance instruments
- ➤ Income and expense budgets
- ➤ Develop a working cure plan leaving it nimble enough to readily change direction in the event of new developments in science, technology or patient care techniques
- ➤ Become a valued and contributing member of the YOPD community as a patient, leader, educator or medical research contributor
- ➤ Write a book
- ➤ Join and attend YOPD support groups in St. Louis and Traverse City
- ➤ Attend summer forum meeting
- ➤ Assist in fundraisers
- ➤ Utilize my technical knowledge, life experiences and business background to create new wave support groups
- ➤ Develop and execute a religious rejuvenation plan
- ➤ Set a meeting with Father Joe
- ➤ Develop a patient care plan, including caregivers, facilities, doctors, insurance plans and medical supply needs

> Define financial constraints and limitations of this plan within defined planning horizons

> Define doctors' list for specific needs and geographic locations

> Fill out and distribute "Oregon Forms"

> Define and begin execution for specific planning horizons

> Develop medical supply acquisitions plan

> Understand types of care facilities and acquisition plans, including personnel, medical and even final resting, if applicable.

> Develop financial and final instruction documents.

KNOW YOUR LIMITATIONS

This is key and in a number of ways I broke the limitations down into people skills, legal background, medical understanding, physical strength, financial understanding, and technical strength, and most importantly, time. You're sick, so remember you may not be as efficient as you used to be. All of us are probably relatively stronger in some areas than in others, and it is important that we accurately assess each of these areas and find ways to shore up our weaknesses. It does not necessarily mean that you must do everything on your own. In fact, this is probably one time in your life where you will need all the help and lucky breaks you can get. One of the most important assessments you will need to make will be to understand the limitations of your plan, especially financially. I found that consistently reviewing your ideas with knowledgeable people in the subject area will increase the accuracy and value of your plan and can be accomplished with little to no cost. Be careful not to overstay your welcome.

UNDERSTANDING YOUR COMPETITION

Yes, there is also competition when it comes to dying. You have heard it before, "He who dies with the most toys wins." Aren't the sport's psychologists who wouldn't let us keep score in our children's T-ball games going to be mad when they find out? It's there though it might be hard to recognize, but pay attention, or they will get you. The word "they" doesn't mean there is someone out there trying to kill you, but refers to the collective distractions that constantly work against your end goal. You know, finding a cure, saving your life. The competition comes from many different places. It competes for your time, your money, your resources, your place in line, and some would argue, your soul, your dignity and even your remains. As in most competition, there is always a winner and a loser based on a defined technique of scoring. In this game you are given a limited set of tools - these being time, resources and money. You win when you accomplish something faster, cheaper or better, thus expending less than someone else does with the ultimate win being that you are cured before you expire. They win when you waste any one of your resources with "their" ultimate win coming when you expire. I would suggest that you think about the rules in which you will play by. I would offer the following suggestions for your consideration:

> There is such a thing as friendly competition. Use it when it makes sense. Remember you are also running in the human

race. Sometimes the greater good need prevail. Understand when it's important and relevant.

➤ Even in defeat, be dignified.

➤ Your competitor is not always well-defined and can often switch teams or play on both sides. Be careful who you trust.

➤ Play by the rules! It's how you will be remembered.

➤ Be respectful of people's time. They will be generous, but do not abuse it.

Let me give you some examples. There was a new drug that had just been released that showed great promise for my condition. It had been approved in Europe and had many success stories. One of the Hospitals that I was dealing with at the time was being compensated to recruit patients for the study. I was the perfect candidate. I should go for it based on what I just told you right? Wrong! What no one was quick to point out was that the drug had been fast-tracked by the FDA and was now available in the U.S. It was expected that study participants commit for up to a year and a half and participants had a 50/50 chance of receiving a placebo. In reality, I could receive the drug now with no chance of a placebo, and if it worked, I would be that much further ahead in receiving at least a little relief from my problem. If I stayed in the program, I could have lost a year and a half if I drew the 50/50 chance of the placebo or I would have had to withdraw from the program in order to be sure I was receiving the drug. The bottom line is that the only winner here would have been the organization that was rewarded for recruiting the candidates.

➢ One example of losing with dignity might be to donate your remains to science in the event that you lose your battle. In PSP research for example, there is a need for brains to be donated post mortem for research purposes. Scientists want to better understand what is causing the disease and what effect it has on its victims and since there does not seem to be a definitive way to diagnose PSP with 100% accuracy without an autopsy, you may finally confirm your diagnosis for the benefit of your heirs. This may work in conjunction with more traditional organ donor programs.

➢ Playing by the rules could be as simple as parking in handicap spots only when you are suffering downtime or feeling "off," and not when you are "on" and really don't need it.

➢ Be careful not to make informal requests of people's time without a need to support it. People are looking for ways to help and will be overly sensitive to doing things to help with your every need.

UNDERSTANDING YOUR NEW FINANCIAL STATEMENT

➢ For those who are experiencing similar situations, you have no doubt realized that your whole world has been turned upside down, and your finances will be no different. It is critical that you get this under control as quickly as possible.

First thing you need to do is grab a calendar, because what you will need to create is a timeline for the various events that will begin to happen over the next couple of days, months, and hopefully years. Just like on the medical side where there are very few cases that look exactly alike, this too will be true on the financial side, as well. Now that you have a calendar, you can start doing your research to determine what kind of shape you are really in. Whether you have done advanced planning with a certified financial planner or are totally ill-prepared, there will be surprises when you get right down to it. I would suggest that you gather up all of your information and review it all line by line to make sure you understand the details. In my case, quick action and turnaround on the paperwork was worth over 33% increase per month for the rest of my life. This was because of the way my company figures their long-term disability benefits. In another matter, it was worth another 25% per month. **Lesson Learned** - understanding the rules and making sure they work in your favor can be very valuable.

➢ Another key thought process you will need to get used to is "innocent until proven guilty." You will find that the insurance company's motto will read "healthy until proven sick" over a long period of time. During that period, expect there to be many traps designed to limit the financial commitment and assistance of your insurance company. The traps may lurk in paperwork deadlines, stepping payment programs, limits on total payouts and multiple verifications of your illness. You will come to realize that finding a good physician is not only measured by how technically qualified they are, but also by how savvy their office staff are at handling the demanding paperwork processes the insurance company will put them through. This is tough for most offices, because it is hard to tie revenue to the work created. Your Human Resource Specialist and Social Security Coordinator will become your new best friends, because chances are, if you work for a company with good benefits, even those will be coordinated along with other sources of income to limit the amount of money you can make to two-thirds of your current income. Don't panic just yet, as this may not be as bad as it sounds, because some of the income you may start receiving may be tax free due the taxation laws involving income from insurance policies. In general, if you have a policy that pays you a benefit, the portion of the policy that is not paid by your company is usually non taxable. The end goal is to produce your new P&L to see where you stand. First, do this for the short-term picture (6-12 months). Later in the book, we will begin producing plans based on your long-term planning horizons.

UNDERSTANDING YOUR SOURCES OF INCOME

Let me start by saying that I was extremely lucky to be working for a caring and generous corporation in EMC and lucky that I had, for reasons unknown to me, decided to check a couple of boxes during the benefit enrollment period that resulted in the level of benefits that I am receiving. In addition, my luck continued to show in that the establishment of the benefit amounts ended up being based on one of my higher W2 years ever. Too bad I didn't have the same luck on the health side. **Lesson Learned** - regardless of how healthy you think you are, make sure you have ample financial coverage in case of a disability. You need to very quickly get your information together and figure out where you stand. Even better, since it is probably off hours when you are reading this, see if your company has an on-line tool for information, tracking, application submission and benefit levels. Then contact your Human Resources Group - they will be able to confirm your sources and amounts of income. They will probably include a mix of the following:

Salary extension benefits – Many companies will try to payout a combination of vacation and sick pay prior to getting insurance involved in order to keep their insurance rates low. I found that in many states, you want to avoid this if possible, because if you do end up on short or long-term disability, which effectively separates you from the company, your company will probably pay you off for any unused time at some point in time. In many states, it is the law.

Sick pay – Some companies will institute sick pay policies in order to minimize short-term disability costs, thus keeping the process less formal. I believe this works to your advantage if you never end up on long-term disability. However, if you think you will end up there eventually, make sure you understand the timing of the various policies and the interactions so that there are no filing deadlines missed, and as in my case, that prolonging paperwork doesn't cost you benefits, especially during recessionary times.

Short-term disability - I have found this to be the most costly period to the individual employee, because the benefit is typically the lowest paying part of the policy unless you buy special supplementary insurance. The duration on this policy is usually the shortest, as well, which is the good news. I believe 6-12 weeks covers most plans. However, if you still have the luxury of affecting your planning horizons, make sure your savings can cover this transition period.

Long-term disability- This is the big one in many cases, especially when a disease like Parkinson's shows up. My particular policy could payout for as many as 20.5 years based on my age at disability and Social Security's definition of retirement for my age group. Buy all of this you can get and don't worry if your company is not subsidizing it, as it will only work to your advantage from a taxable income perspective if you pay the premiums. **Lesson Learned** – double check the contribution percentage that your company reports to the LTD insurance carrier and eventually to the IRS. It appears that my company figured a company average when the policy was established, and since the majority of the claims seemed to be coming from the secretarial staff for maternity leave, the contribution percentages were skewed to favor the lower paid employees. After some research on the subject, I was able to get EMC to change my contribution percentage to reflect the real numbers for me, and not the company average. This changed my taxable income percentage from 64% to 41%, and I will continue to argue that it should still be lowered to approximately 31% - in other words, huge tax savings for me and the company. So you guys in accounting go down and talk to your Human Resources group and check it out. I think if they did it right, it could have been worth some real money, by my standards anyway.

Life insurance benefits – There are a number of things that we need to consider here. First of all, most people have term life policies through work. They are the cheapest and most effective way to solve the life insurance problem. What most people do not realize is that many companies have invested in the option of converting the policy upon disability to a whole life policy with waiver of premiums paid until retirement age. If this is the case with your company, make sure you understand the tax implications on payout. Some companies even have clauses that allow early payouts if terminal illness is diagnosed. The payout is usually discounted at a pretty steep rate, but at least you get some control over how it is used and may finally see something positive out of the premiums you've paid.

Social Security benefits for disability or retirement – Six months to the day your disability begins, you will be eligible for Social Security benefits provided you have made the qualifying hurdles. You can check with Social Security to see what your benefit would be. It is also probably the hardest money to earn if you don't keep on top of the paperwork, which is what I had been told. It is important, however, that these applications get done correctly - not only the first time but throughout the renewal checks, as well. Many of you will find that other insurance companies will follow the lead of the SSA for qualifying, as well as setting retirement dates and cost of living adjustments. So if Social Security ever suspends your payments, be ready for the rest of them to be affected as well. For me, this process seemed to be a very positive one. Dr. Bruining knew the importance of the timing for me and had plenty of experience in filling out the paperwork. I set up a meeting with my case coordinator so I could be face to face with him, and he could see how my Parkinson's affected my life in sales. All in all, I received approval in just over three weeks from the time I began my process, and to their credit, once SSA and the Traverse City office received my paperwork, it took approximately a week and a half to receive approval. My long-term disability company was floored when they called to offer legal help in getting through the process, which I thought was mighty nice of them, and then I realized that once SSA was approved they got to reduce their payments to me by that amount. Now I understand the compassion. A couple of points to consider and remember:

➢ SSA payments can be taxable depending upon your other sources and amounts of income.

➢ Your SSA payments may be reduced if you earn other income. Make sure you understand the impact of taking a part-time or second replacement job before you start spending that new paycheck.

➢ SSA offers many benefits for those looking to find work that they can perform. These additional benefits include job placement services and retraining assistance.

I am going to set up an appointment with SSA to figure out if I am getting myself in trouble by writing this book. So far, I am receiving no pay for anything I am doing nor do I have either a degree or any formal training in any of the fields covered in this book, and so getting someone to hire me based on a "trust me" concept is unlikely, and I still continue to qualify for total disability based upon all of the tests. I am questioning how it will be handled so stay tuned by visiting the web site when it goes live. I do hope to someday turn this into a modest income, as I do still have two kids in college and an ex-wife on the payroll. One of my open issues will be to figure out the impact.

Long-term care benefits – Buying this insurance policy a couple of years ago was the best investment I ever made. If you are lucky enough to work for a company that allows you to buy a standard or buy-up plan for LTD, take it. In fact, put this book down and go figure out how you can sign up for it if you haven't already. These policies are all over the map in terms of what and how long they will payout so understand what you are getting. In my case, it will pay until one of the following events happens:

➢ I am no longer disabled in my profession. Make sure this clause exists so that you don't go on disability as a doctor and come back at the salary of a general laborer.

➢ I reach SSA defined retirement age of 76 ½. (I was 46 when diagnosed with my disability.)

➢ I expire (then my estate would receive two extra monthly payments.)

Most policies are based on your previous earning year or years. Mine was based on the last year. I have talked to others that have one that averages the last three years. This could work for or against you, I suppose, but in recessionary times, and especially the beginning, I will bet the one-year plan works to your advantage. There are a few other key provisions that you may want to look for in a policy, which are as follows:

➤ Some policies will allow you to earn up to your old salary amount without penalty. The equation would be Old Salary – LTD amount (66 2/3%) = amount you can earn without penalty to your LTD benefit amount.

➤ Check to see if there is a COLA adjustment annually.

➤ Make sure you understand what the annual qualifying requirements are and have your doctors ready for their part.

➤ **Catastrophic insurance** – This insurance was part of my LTD coverage I did not originally quality for, and it is so easily overlooked. You usually have to take a skills assessment test to qualify. In my case, I had to fail in three out of five categories of daily functions. The interesting thing here with Parkinson's patients is to not assume that you must be dysfunctional 100% of the time. As we are all too well aware, depending on your "on" and "off" periods, your daily abilities' test results may vary by the hour. My insurance carrier was looking for proof that my condition caused me problems enough so that I required assistance on a regular basis.

➤ **Local charities and support groups** – There are some out there. Your first step here may be to find a local support group. They usually have the best handle on where to find the money. There are also many sources available on the web. There seems to be a number of programs out there that assist in Respite Care or Drug Assistance Programs.

➤ **Health insurance** - This is one that is still somewhat of a puzzle. EMC has been generous enough to cover our insurance needs until Medicare kicks in for me. My wife, Melanie, had insurance through her employer and EMC for a while, but she lost her insurance when she had to quit and start taking care of me full-time. Once I have been receiving Social Security for 24 months (March 2009), I will be eligible to receive Medicare benefits. However, Medicare will only cover me and not Melanie, and so we will have to obtain a health insurance plan for her. The other subject that needs to be explored is which plan to take for the supplemental insurance or Medicare Part D.

➤ **401K and IRA retirement plans** - Depending on your prognosis, these may be worth looking into, especially if it looks like you may never reach normal retirement age. Remember to consider the tax implications, because if you are considered fully disabled, you can at least avoid the 10% penalty for early withdrawal. If the withdrawal happens close to the year-end time frame, you may want to consider in which year you want to attribute the extra income, since your taxable rates will probably be lower in the years you are on disability. This is one of those last resort ideas in most cases, because you are essentially betting against yourself that you will make it to retirement age to be able to collect this money. Talk to your accountant if you have one, and get their advice on the consequences.

➢ **Equity in your personal property** – This would include things like reverse equity loans or sale or disposal of other assets, i.e., vacation homes, old cars, boats, etc.

➢ **Previous equity investments** – In this exercise, you would want to study closely from a tax perspective such investments as coin collections, stamp collections, stocks and/or bonds and stock grants or options.

➢ **Allowable second incomes** - Be careful to understand the impact on your health, as well as your pocket book. There are many formulas involved, and I must confess I still don't understand mine as well as I need to.

➢ **Social Security disability** - In most cases the SSA encourages getting you back to work, but there are offsets to the monthly checks you receive.

➢ **LTD policy** - As with Social Security, there may be situations where money you earn may be offset from your disability check. Some policies do allow a second income up to a limit without penalty.

Now you need to gather all of your information so that you can begin to develop your planning horizons. Here is the real trick, because you are laying out planning horizons, and you have to make an educated guess as to how long you are going to live. There are very few doctors that are going to give you a day and time for your demise, as there are just too many unknowns from day to day that can change to work for you or against you. So, you see the problem here. If the doctor cannot predict anything based on what they have seen, then how much more accurate can you be? Ironically, a strong contingency plan is a must, especially if you live beyond your expectations. My plan looks pretty good until age 76.5, and then I have some holes to plug if I make it. That will be a welcome problem to deal with between now and then.

My biggest **Lesson Learned** – The EMC Human Resources group has been invaluable to me during this process. I will continue to trust and confide in them, because their assistance has greatly aided me in being able to present to you a very positive financial outcome, instead of how to effectively fight off bankruptcy and avoid creditors. I will continue to double check every piece of advice and information given to me to make sure of its accuracy and pertinence to my situation.

I would also make one recommendation at this point to Jack and his crew based on my experience, and that is to put someone or some organization in place to help people like me through the process when it looks like the end result may be to file a disability claim. It gets quite complicated, and I do not believe that the level of expertise nor the availability of the existing Human Resources counselors are at the level they should be with the complexity of the insurance contracts that exist, and a mistake early on would be very costly. This could be handled in a number of ways - either through a support group of employees willing to serve in that capacity or the addition of a staff person solely dedicated to assist in these situations. I would start their training with a thorough review of the benefits' environment to see if there are any other hidden surprises out there like the two or three that I have found. They may also want to revisit cases of employees like me who went on leave before I found the problem to see if they can still recoup some of the money for that employee, as well as for the company. Another option would be to have the Benefits' Department schedule a round table meeting with the employee and their spouse or significant other to review the situation and make recommendations on how to proceed as a team. As you can see, there are many decisions that should be made, but only after you have developed a thorough understanding of all of the benefit options that will affect you. With the complexity added when you look at tax ramifications and Medicare options, as well as a spousal situation for respite care, the possibilities are unlimited. Although all of these are good ideas, they should never replace the top priority of educating the employees on what they have prior to anything happening so that none of this is a surprise. I would be happy to help start the support group option and see if there are other employees that would like to participate.

UNDERSTANDING YOUR EXPENSES

Your expense picture will change mostly in a negative way, but there are a couple of things worth looking into, which include the following:

Many life insurance policies have a conversion or waiver of premium clause should you become disabled. Check this out fairly quickly, as you will need to protect this benefit, if it applies, for two reasons. One - since you now have a record of having a chronic illness, you will be, at best, inhibited in acquiring any new life insurance. Two - your policy will now begin paying for itself so you will probably gain a couple hundred dollars a month in savings.

Government backed student loans have a disability clause that suspends payments in the event of a disability. However, this only applies if you are the responsible party and not just the co-signer.

Many credit cards will offer you an insurance policy that will suspend payments while you are disabled. Although this sounds good when you first hear it, in my opinion, it is a scam. The credit card company only makes the minimum payment, which is often less than the monthly finance charge. So, if this is true, you may end up owing more at the end of your disability then when you started.

With many chronic illnesses, they eventually become debilitating in some way. Your doctor may be required to report your medical condition to the Department of Motor Vehicles' in your state, which could result in the loss or suspension of your license. If this should happen and you are a multiple-vehicle family, you may want to sell one of more of your vehicles as a means of savings. In our household, I only drive in case of an emergency, and since we generally lease our cars, we are cutting down to one car. By doing this, we will eliminate a car payment, as well as the associated operational costs and insurance.

The only other expenses that will change in a beneficial manner are those related to work. My dry cleaning expense has gone down to almost nothing, and lunch expenses and miscellaneous employee non reimbursable travel no longer exists.

On the other hand, your medical expenses will obviously increase considerably. There are some steps to take to reduce the impact, which include the following:

➢ If you have a health plan with a FSA or HSA account, make sure that you are contributing the maximum amount allowable. This will allow you to maximize your taxable income scenarios.

➢ Review your medical options for health insurance during the open enrollment period. There may be a plan that better suits your new situation. Lower family maximums or personal deductibles are probably going to work for your family. Also, make sure that the policy you choose does not have a limit if you can avoid it.

➢ In most cases you are now on a fixed income so prudent spending applies.

HAVE A PLAN FOR WHEN YOU ARE GONE

If you follow steps similar to those outlined in this book, you will spend a significant amount of time preparing all of the plans and documents required to put a plan in place. Make sure you have someone that understands the intricacies of your plan. There are a number of things you may want to consider while making these plans.

If you have a complex estate, then you may want to hire a consultant to work with your executor toward the completion of your estate plan. I would use the word complex as a relative word here, as it may be complex financially or from a relationship standpoint or both. My particular plan will involve a combined family, including six kids, a wife and an ex-wife, six grandkids, two homes in two different states, three vacation time shares with an estate value that closely follows the ever increasing maximum amount that allows you exemption from paying the inheritance tax. On the debt side, it is fairly clean with the exception of my mortgages, automobile and student loans. Once again, I am very fortunate, because I have close family members whose professions are those of CPA's, bankers, lawyers, and psychologists. The question is, do I want to burden family members with cleaning up my mess? I have adopted a rule that if I use these resources, I will have the estate pay them for their time. I would suggest that you review these decisions from an economic, limitation and conflict of interest standpoint.

My plan will allow for a lawyer, CPA, financial planner, a spiritual advisor and perhaps a therapist to deal with my estate issues. I have always assumed that if you want to reveal the vulnerable side of family members, friends or acquaintances then watch how they react when the will is read. I have shared my financial wishes with my kids, wife and ex-wife ahead of time to minimize problems when the time comes. I believe I now know where the land mines are, but only time will tell. Just as in most business deals, the fairest and most equitable deals are the ones where no one is totally happy with the results. As with all other facets of the plan, you may want to create a list of goals and objectives for how you want future decisions to be made. It may look something like this:

➤ Ensure that there is ample money available to cover your spouse or significant other's daily living expenses within reason.

➤ Strive to create a plan that that will sustain your spouse or significant other until they pass. Beyond that time, ensure that your assets will be divided equitably amongst your children.

➤ Minimize the impact of federal taxes on estate balances.

➤ Distribute as much money to your kids as quickly as possible without compromising goals one and two.

➤ Minimize administrative expenses as much as possible.

➤ Maintain a semi-conservative investment strategy.

DEVELOP PLANNING HORIZONS

This chapter, from a financial standpoint, may be one of the most important exercises in this book, because it is aimed at helping you develop financial planning horizons associated with your life stages, and it exposes weaknesses in your current retirement plan. I have broken my plan down into four sections, because it seemed to follow the major changes in benefit levels that are associated with my life situation. My definition of a "planning horizon" is a period of years grouped together by a theme or status in life. Since most of us will hopefully retire and receive Social Security benefits, in my case at age 76 ½ had I not gotten ill, a plan pre and post retirement age usually makes sense.

If you are married or have children that you plan to provide for upon your death, then a plan that covers the period after your death also makes sense. In this case, make sure that it is consistent with your Will or Trust so there is no conflict. Your horizons may be different based on your specific goals in life. I have a friend who swears he will retire before he is 55, as his father passed away at a younger age from a disease that is known to be genetic, and he figures his demise may come at an earlier age, as well. So his planning horizon will be different than mine in that he will need to address two more periods of time, i.e., the period during which he is still working, as well as the period which addresses income levels he will need from age 55 through 67 ½. Likewise, if you are still working, you may need a plan from now until you become totally disabled or retire. Remember, this plan is easier when done prior to being diagnosed with a terminal or chronic illness, and so if you are reading this book for the benefit of another individual, ask yourself how it applies to you. If I would have completed the exercise a little earlier in my life, I may have added some additional themes a little more formally, such as the college years or the single years between marriages or the alimony years - you get the point. The horizons that seemed logical for me at this stage are:

> ➤ Disabled pre retirement benefits, age 49-76 ½

> ➤ Disabled post retirement benefits, age 76 ½ and beyond

> ➤ Disabled pre retirement benefits for my wife and kids in case of death, present to age 76 ½

> ➤ Disabled post retirement benefits, age 76 ½ and beyond

> ➤ Disabled pre retirement benefits, age 49-76 ½

This plan should be as unique as a fingerprint in that it will probably be made up of a mix of Social Security and LTD policies, potentially a spouse's income and/or miscellaneous income generated from hobbies or investments. There may also be a section that accounts for miscellaneous life insurance benefits if you happen to have a whole life insurance policy. The key to success here is that you must look at the various retirement dates, anniversary dates and effective dates that may leave gaps in your financial plan. You still often have an option at this point to enhance your normal retirement years through contributions to IRAs, etc., often through a spouse or significant other's plan. Take the opportunity if you get it, as Lady Luck may swing in your favor, and you may well need it.

DISABLED POST RETIREMENT 76 ½ AND BEYOND

This plan typically includes your 401ks and Social Security Administration checks, plus payouts from retirement plans. Since we have been robbing this fund because of the health situation I am in, we will need to build on the assets to make this plan consistent all the way through my wife's golden years.

Disabled pre retirement benefits for my wife and kids in case of death, now to age 76 ½

In my case, this plan shifts entirely from a monthly-funded income and insurance check to a lump sum deposit for which to live off the principle and investment income stream. It is key that you ensure that you have ample insurance proceeds or bank deposits to fund the lifestyle you are projecting. This may change drastically if the economy shifts to a recessionary economy and investment returns are minimized.

Succession and progression planning

Once again, all the planning in the world does you no good if you don't have anyone to administrate it! Choosing the right trustee or administrator is crucial. Be sure you choose someone who will look out for the interests of all concerned per your instructions and treat all beneficiaries equally. This may be a family member or a hired investment counselor, etc. In my experience, the key factors to consider when choosing an estate administrator are as follows:

➢   Ability to deal with a multi-faceted group of individuals who may, at times, have competing goals

➢   Investment experience

➢   Both tax and budgeting experience

My timeline to date

- ➤ July 2005 – diagnosed with sleep apnea; had surgery on tonsils, soft pallet and uvula by local ENT doctor

- ➤ November 2005- saw doctor's local ENT, local sleep doctor, local Family Practice and local Endo; diagnosed with diabetes and sleep apnea again; began taking Metaforin and using CPAP machine at an 8 setting

- ➤ January 5, 2006 – woke up in the morning with my arm asleep; when it woke up, I no longer had full use of it; it appeared to others as if I was favoring it in that is was in a protective mode at all times and somewhat cocked

- ➤ January 2006 - saw doctor/internist at Family Practice; my GP began testing for heart problems and signs of stroke, which included a stress test; all tests came back normal

- ➤ January 2006 – saw local neuromuscular doctor for a nerve test (EMG)

- ➤ February 2006 – referred to local neurosurgeon who ordered an MRI to look for a tumor; tests came back normal by his standards

- ➤ February 2006 – follow-up visit with local Neurosurgeon, Barber and local Endo; no real progress except to rule out heart, lung, cancer issues

- ➤ April 2006 – began working with my urologist for bladder and ED issues

- ➤ May 2006 – first visit to Dr. Bruining, a neurologist who diagnoses some form of Parkinson's; suggests I get second opinion, because it doesn't look typical; said she suspected PSP; I went home and did some reading and booked an appointment with the Mayo Clinic in Rochester, Minnesota

➢ May 2006 – contacted Human Resource Group at EMC

➢ June-July 2006 - follow-up visits with Dr. Bruining, local Endo, local neuromuscular and local Family Practice; looks like sugar or diabetic symptoms are disappearing, but growth hormones and testosterone levels are out of line; bladder problems continue to increase

➢ August 2006 – First trip to Mayo Clinic in Rochester; when I called to schedule the appointment, the scheduler decided that my diabetic problems would have to be addressed first, and so she assigned me to the Endocrinology Department. Once I presented my symptoms to the intake doctor, he scheduled numerous tests and also tried to book me with the Neurology Department with some success. Mayo's initial diagnosis was Parkinson's, but further defined it as PSP. I scheduled my second trip for September. I was asked to begin taking a new drug called Azilect with a dosage of .5mg at Mayo. Mayo would not prescribe it, as they had not ever had any experience working with it. Azilect became FDA approved in May 2006. (This is the drug mentioned earlier in the book as a research project that I turned down because it is readily available). Dr. Bruining in Traverse City agreed to let me try it (again taking control of your care) after I showed her detailed information on the benefits of this drug. It worked great to give me additional dopamine increases for about a year and half, and then I started to get to where I couldn't eat anything with protein in it without feeling nauseated. I switched to Zelapar at a dosage of 1.25, and I have been on this medication for eight months so far, and it is working well for me. Again, take control of your situation. The insurance company wanted me to try a cheaper version, but this did not work for me, and so Dr.

Bruining contacted them, and they approved my taking Zelapar.

➤ September 2006 – began experiencing both increased urinary and ED issues; saw URI doctor; began taking both Detrol and Cialis; stopped the Detrol pretty quickly after I started taking it, as it had no effect. Afterward, it was discovered that over-active bladder was not the problem, but rather, it was incomplete empting that was causing the frequency issues.

➤ November 2006 – follow-up trip to Mayo; numerous tests associated with neurology and urology; notable results included incomplete bladder drainage; began having to use catheter and showing signs of autonomic problems brewing; ED problems increased; Cialis is no longer working; started on a special mix called TRIMIX (see TMI Section for more detail)

➤ October 2006 – short-term disability started from EMC; initiated paperwork process for SSA

➤ December 29, 2006 – retired from EMC on disability

➤ February 2007 – first check arrived for long-term disability at the end of the month (plan accordingly for one month of short funds)

➤ March 2007 – started doing research on writing a book and deciding on format

➤ April 2007 – received first SSA check (one month behind March 2007 start time)

➤ May 2007 – played golf with Mike T., and came up with the idea for the book

- June 2007 - traveled to Mayo Clinic again; met with Dr. Feeley, who again confirmed the suspected PSP diagnosis

- July 2007 – attended summer forum meeting in Traverse City and a side meeting with representatives of NIH; had lunch with NIH staff and was invited out to Washington, D.C. for further testing and diagnosis

- October 2007 – went to NIH in early October and discovered a study being run by Dr. Litvan in Louisville at the same time. Since Dr. Litvan ran the Neurological Movement Disorder program at NIH, they immediately recommended that I see her; went to Louisville at the end of the month and met with Dr. Litvan, who changed my diagnosis to MSA; she had me stop taking the Azilect and started me on Zelapar

- February 2008 - began construction on the new house in St. Louis

- March 2008 – second trip to see Dr. Litvan; disease had progressed to the point where every three hours, I was going through a cycle of almost normal functioning to being bedridden taking only the Parcopa; she suggested that I check into the hospital and go through a medicine effectiveness study for one week

- April 2008 – started to have balance issues and began falling down; had a reunion with my longtime high school friends at the Kingsley Club; began writing the Kingsley Club story as a gift to Ed for his generosity over the last couple of years

- May 2008 – checked in at Frasier Rehab Clinic for a one week evaluation; changed the complete medication routine and began some physical and occupational therapy; started serious work on the book, as well as many of the resulting projects

➢ June 2008 – got most of my strength issues worked out with the medication changes, but started experiencing balance issues; thought that was an okay trade, but now I am beginning to wonder; the balance problems are increasing, as is the need for additional Sinemet

➢ July 2008 - fell numerous times resulting in broken ribs and hand; began the search for new doctors in St Louis; hired cousin Karen to begin working with Melanie on decorating the house; did final inspection on July 16, and we are closing on the July 29; on July 30, we have approximately 12 different contractors coming over to the house for various reasons; I need to line up people and materials for the week Dave, Kim and the boys are in town so I can keep them all busy. I will probably require a tracheotomy if things keep progressing like they are; still keeping hope that the experimental Botox procedure will work, although the doctors are now in a split decision as to how effective it will be; my conservative ENT in Traverse City says I should do it now. Since I am typing this on a plane at the moment returning from visiting our new granddaughter in Monterey and my vocal cords are singing, I am sure that most of my fellow passengers would agree with Dr. Collins; I view this as a last resort in solving this problem.

➢ August 2008 - began the moving process to St Louis; applying for a study through Washington University that will test a new Sinemet delivery system; looking at options for maintaining a relationship with the Frazier Clinic through my doctor.

> September 2008 – They were right, I did need a Tracheostomy! Wasn't exactly an emergency but was a definite necessity. A pulmonary Embolism in my lung sidelined me almost permanently. Note even if you have a passion to write, or paint or whatever do it in moderation to make sure you move, sitting in one place a long time and the combination of falling, caused these blood clots which moved from my legs to my lungs. This, with a combination of weak vocal cords, made it necessary to get the trach. I have been in the hospital for a week in ER, ICU and surgery recovery. I have just moved to the rehab floor to get my strength back and my independence. My progress is coming along nicely; the staff here at Munson Hospital has been fantastic. Again take control of your health care, ask questions and always refuse tests or medications if you are not sure why they are necessary. These can be added later once you understand why. If you are told to discontinue your medications for any reason, call your neurologist immediately, when the neurologist on call tried to discontinue all of my medications because I was having surgery saying it would not cause any reaction to stop them and start them later, (it will) my wife called Dr. Bruining and mentioned all of my meds were being stopped, she stepped in and within 10 minutes I had my medications. Do not be afraid to supersede the staff and go to someone who knows your circumstances.   All the nurses to respiratory to the Doctors who have painstakingly answered all of my and my wife's questions. I had a tube in my throat and then surgery for the trach, it was hard to get my wife and my guests to understand what I wanted, and they tried charades, a dry erase board and a process of elimination. I will have to tell them how far off they really were in interpretation but their hearts were in it.

TMI

Let me start this section with an apology and a warning. The apology is to all my fellow victims who may disagree with my style of writing or the candid nature of this chapter. Believe me, I thought long and hard about how to write this section before I chose this style. I finally chose this style, because the other styles that I contemplated were either too dry to read and not lose interest, too technical for the lay person to understand, or too depressing for both the author to write and relive and the reader to read and either relive or look forward to. I will also apologize to any reader that finds talk about male sexual functions and male psychology offensive. If this is the case, then I would suggest skipping this chapter and read the rest of the book, as it will stand on its own. Then, if you wish, come back and read this section. This way, if you find it offensive, you will still get the benefit of the PG-13 section.

If you decide to go ahead then there are a couple of rules. You will notice if you have a hardcover version of this book that this chapter has a seal that you will need to break in order to read it. Since I have a technical and software background, I couldn't resist adding the following comment: "By breaking this seal, you agree to the terms and conditions described in this chapter." But first, a couple more points. The idea for the style was sparked while watching last comic standing. I dedicate this chapter to Josh Blue, a Cerebral Palsy victim, whom I believe is not only absolutely hysterical as a standup comedian, but I sense through actions and routines in his act that he is a very brave and courageous person. So, the rules that you must agree to are as follows:

- You cannot laugh at me or any of the characters in my stories - you must laugh with us. Failure to do so will result in you going straight to JAIL - not passing go and not collecting $200 dollars.

- If you decide to try some of the ideas in this chapter and you experience a similar or funny situation, you must share it with others. You can do this by logging on to our website and entering your story under the story time section. In other words, do not try this at home. We take no responsibility for your actions, especially if you end up as a Darwin award candidate.

- If you decide that some of the home recipes seem like something you want to try, please seek the advice of your doctor first to see if they might have any objections.

- Since I am currently retired or disabled and unable to work a "normal" job, I am constantly looking for productive ways to spend my time that result in the advancement of the goals and objectives outlined above. So, if this turns into a second career for me as a standup comedian or a YouTube star, please vote for me when it seems appropriate.

- Pity parties are not allowed. Those of us that are dealing with the diseases have to adopt a whole new logic and attitude to get by. There can be no regression. This chapter will introduce some grassroots wisdom to many of you. Sayings like, "If you think suffering from Parkinson's is a long, slow death, I say try living to 100" will be common.

> ➢ There can be no retribution for any of the characters in this chapter. The situations described may be slightly embellished for comedic value and names may be changed to protect the innocent and to keep me from being sued!

> ➢ If you catch yourself laughing or breaking any of the rules listed above or you just want to support the cause, then you must log on to our website and go to the pay fine section and pay what you can afford. The proceeds will be split based on the policies found on the website. (Allen Cullen, if you are out there reading this and laughing, you owe me a "hundo," as this idea was inspired by your management meetings in the good old days.)

> ➢ Finally, I say thank you to my wife for letting me share with you some of the most intimate details of our life. I have never been one to kiss and tell, but here I think it is appropriate.

OVERVIEW OF THE SITUATION

I must start this section by describing the disease as my body has defined it. As many of you know, almost every case of Parkinson's is different. In fact, I would describe the disease as a collection of symptoms that have been banded together and called Parkinson's, because there is no other disease that will claim them. The things that these symptoms do have in common are that they are all neurological with many of them being caused by an imbalance of dopamine somewhere in the brain, and it is the dopamine that allows the neurons in the brain to talk to the muscles that they control. The portion of the brain that is affected will control how the disease progresses throughout the body and the time progression it follows.

The diagnosis of Parkinson's is subjective in that there is no exact test that they run that definitively diagnoses Parkinson's. In fact, I think it fair to say that it's a diagnosis by elimination. In my case and many others that I know of, there has been a history of diagnoses that were either later clarified as a different sub-class of Parkinson's or a different disease all together. That is why you must never give up or become complacent with this disease. It seems that every time I think I have something under control, something changes to render that solution either useless or unnecessary. Most people, when referring to Parkinson's, are probably really talking about a collection of definitions that may also be called Parkinson's Plus Disease. They include an alphabet soup of acronyms including Progressive Supra Nuclear Palsy (PSP), Multi System Atrophy (MSA) and its sub categories of: Olivopontocerebellar Atrophy (OCPA), Striato-Nigral Degeneration (SND), Shy-Drager Syndrome (SDS), Cortical Basal Ganglionic Degeneration (CDBG) and Essential Tremor (ET). Further research on these conditions will provide you greater definition.

Lesson Learned: All the websites you may research contain very scientific information and can be very confusing if you know nothing of the disease. This, combined with an alphabet soup list of acronyms, has the potential of confusing your loved ones and friends as you attempt to explain your diagnosis, especially if you have a Young Onset situation.

I remember when I was going through my diagnosis phase I had called my daughter, Julie. Keep in mind that it was and still is a very emotional time for Julie, and we were both on cell phones a couple of hundred miles apart and in our cars. So, you might imagine the quality of the conversation. Well, the bottom line is that she heard the Shy Drager diagnosis and went home to read about it. She "Googled" it, and the definition was even scarier, because it made a statement that she interpreted as saying that it is a genetic condition commonly found in families from the German territories surrounding Worms or Alsace Loraine, and that it was usually terminal within a very short period of time. As you can imagine, this sent shock waves through the family, and the phones started ringing.

So back to the **Lesson Learned** – First, make it a priority to share the news with your loved ones in person. If that is not possible, I would suggest that you put something in writing and send it to them so they have some notes to reinforce their memory, and when they talk to other family members, they can speak to the facts of your situation and not averages based on a population group that may be quite older than you. Secondly, look for a web site that best fits your needs for this situation and direct them to this site for further information. There are many sites out there, including our own. I will make a list of the best reference sites and their stated intentions on the website so that we can keep it current. Our site name at the time we published this book was www.parkinsonsMSAsupport.com. Below are a few others that are pretty reliable.

Sources of Information

Organization and Contact Information	Services and Information Provided
The National Parkinson Foundation, Inc. www.parkinson.org 1-800-327-4545	This is the largest group out there focused on PD for patients and their loved ones. They provide the latest information to keep you up to speed on new research, events and support groups.
Michael J. Fox Foundation for Parkinson's Research www.michaeljfox.org 1-800-708-7644	Michael has PD. He started this group to teach patients and caregivers about living with PD. They also have a newsletter and a website to keep you up to speed on what is going on.
The Mohammad Ali Parkinson Center www.maprc.com 1-602-406-4931 info@maprc.com	Muhammad Ali has PD. He started The Muhammad Ali Parkinson Center (MAPC), which is a National Parkinson Foundation Center and a great resource for people with PD and their families.
100 Questions and Answers about Parkinson's Disease. Written by Dr. Abraham Lieberman. Available through www.amazon.com	This is one of the easiest to use quick reference guides that I have found in print. It is written in words you can understand, and it is thorough enough to be very useful.

In my case I, seem to have a combination of several of the alphabet soup acronyms stated above. In fact, if I look back at the various diagnoses that I have had, they include Parkinson's, PSP and MSA or Shy Drager. The major issues that I will talk about in this chapter will be the symptoms that have appeared over the last two plus years and the progression I have seen to date. My current working diagnosis is MSA. Now as I think back, in some cases I may have noticed symptoms prior to the diagnosis, but at the time they just seemed like a bunch of unrelated events. It is here I will begin my story of progression. I will continue to update and add to this section in future updates.

So there I was living life to the fullest, as usual, burning the candle at both ends, working hard and playing hard – okay, enough of the clichés. I had been on a twenty plus year run with some of the renown "IT" companies in the business working for the likes of EDS, EMC on the fortune 500 list, being actively involved in three different internet startups, serving as mayor pro-tem of Superior, Colorado during the time it was one of the fastest growing communities in the U.S., raising four kids and coaching their respective baseball and basketball teams. I was moving up the pyramid, just about to declare victory over the self-esteem level and continue working on the self-actualization level. You know the pyramid if you took any kind of psychology class - Maslow's Pyramid of Basic Human Needs. Maslow is the guy who back in the 40's came up with the chart shown below explaining his theories on how human nature develops, and the priority of needs that most human beings require and the typical evolution in which they develop. Note that this is my definition based on what I have learned from a number of sources. This type of definition usually resembles one developed by committee.

(If you are my former professor from Michigan State University and you agree with my definition, please change my grade to an A on my transcripts. You originally gave me a D on this section. If you disagree with my definition, then I probably deserved it. If you would like to change my definition, please send me an email, and I will incorporate with proper credits to the next edition. If you are a psychologist and you like it, please sign on to our website and praise us wildly in the feedback section. If you disagree, then leave your definition on the website, and we will look at all of the definitions and incorporate the best into a future update. If you are a patient and you agree with my definition or want to share something, please log-on to our website and do so.)

Maslow's Pyramid of Basic Human Needs:

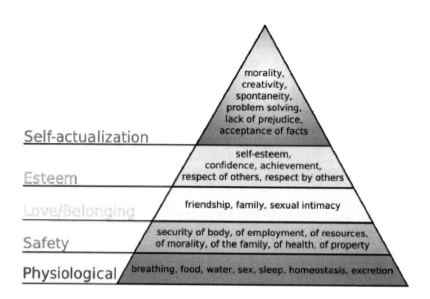

Suddenly, my pyramid started self-destructing before my eyes. They always say that a males sexual function and associated plumbing is the first to go, and guess what? Things started to malfunction. The first symptom was frequent urination to the point where I remember one of my sons asking me if everything was okay after I had excused myself from the table for the fourth time during dinner, only the last time with some urgency. I remember one of those prostate drug commercials playing in my head for a number of days, until I finally got to the urologists office. I fully expected him to tell me that I had a swollen prostate, and that I would be on a lifelong regimen of some BHP drug. Instead I heard,

I cant find anything wrong with the prostate. Lets put you on a drug to relax the bladder - maybe its just overactive. Well, after four weeks with no progress, I determined the fix wasnt working.

At the same time, I was finalizing a divorce, which always divides a family. Although as divorces go, this one was fairly clean, which I now blame on the fact that I probably was suffering from early

Parkinsonism, and was experiencing the symptom that makes you super emotional and lowers your testosterone levels, so you go down with less of a fight. Otherwise, the testosterone may have kicked in, and it might still be unsettled. At the same time, I started putting on some weight and took my first Viagra and was diagnosed with sleep apnea. For the first time in my life, I found myself tearing up watching a "chick flick" other than an *Old Yeller* movie, which, by the way, is one of my favorite *Confederate Railroad* songs, along with *Trashy Women*.

So in a relatively short period of time, I basically wiped out most of the lower three levels of the pyramid and was worried about knocking out the fourth level as well if things didn't start changing. Even still, no one had put any of this together. In fact, I am not sure to this day how much, if not all, is related.

On the bright side, during this same period I met, fell in love with and married my wife, Melanie. I gained two step kids, and soon we will have 6 grandkids (Update: On 7/8/07, Lillie Grace was born to our son, Todd, and his wife Amy.) We relocated to the Traverse City, Michigan area to be near the Kingsley Club, which was a new golf club that a friend of mine had just built. This was a fantastic summer, and my last summer prior to being diagnosed with Parkinson's. I got to play over 100 rounds of golf at the Kingsley Club, a top 20 ranked course according to Golf Week and other courses around the country. One of the advantages of golfing in northern Michigan, especially at the Kingsley Club, is that it is light until almost 10:30 p.m. during the months of June and July. This meant I could put in a full day's work and be on the tees and still get in 18 holes or whatever I felt like. I would carry my cell phone with me, and my sales reps that I worked with knew it was no problem to call me late into the evening, because they knew they would catch me on the golf course. I met some new friends and neighbors in northern Michigan, I was killing my sales numbers, and I got to enjoy free concerts at Interlochen Music Camp almost every night of the week, as the music echoed from across the lake. I suppose this is not what the psychologists meant when they tell you to try and live a balanced life, but my life has always been like this. Even when I was a kid, there weren't enough hours in the day. My credo was to live everyday like it was my last and to work hard and play harder. Who knows, maybe I have always known deep down inside that there was something wrong, and I didn't want to miss anything in a short life scenario.

So, I am writing this section of the book on May 8, 2008, sitting in a hospital bed in Louisville, Kentucky. It has been more than two years since symptoms first presented. We have traveled the world since then searching for a cure and checking off things on our list of 10,000 things we want to do before we die, many of which include golf and travel. We keep on expanding the number, feeling like it might extend things a bit, because those of you that know me know that I do not like t o leave things undone. Although my condition continues to decline, we seem to have at least slowed it down a little and have found ways to correct some of the issues through the wonders of science. It is here I will start to share some of the lessons in life I am learning.

You Say I Got What!!

Don't think that just because you have Parkinson's your libido shuts down in conjunction with your ability to perform sexually. I have found, in fact, that you probably think of it more often and crave it even more. I had read one psychologist's article that hinted that your desire probably increases, because you are feeling vulnerable about life, and human nature dictates that you were placed on this earth to procreate and extend your contribution to the human DNA progression. The logic follows that it would drive you to think about mating all the time, since your time is limited. Well, it's not that bad, but I will admit that I would probably respond "Making Love to my wife!" or "Playing Golf with my grown children or grandchildren!" if asked how I would like to die. The only negative in that wish is the consideration of how those scenarios might psychologically affect my wife or children if it were to happen that way.

I remember hearing a story about a guy in the London area who was terminally ill. I do not remember what he had, but I think it was heart related. At any rate, he knew he had little time to live and was alone and moderately rich by London standards. Well, he ran an advertisement stating that he would reward the last woman who was successful in making love to him by making her the beneficiary of his estate, estimated to be worth over 100,000 British pounds. At today's exchange rates, that's more than $200,000. His plan worked like a charm, and for a short time he created a steady stream of suitors and was living out his dream, until Scotland Yard found out when a line of fine looking, young women formed outside his London apartment, one of which told a local constable what was going on. Well, after much debate, they decided that he should be charged with soliciting a prostitute, effectively shutting him down. This guy understood all aspects of human nature, and in a very immoral way, he helped prove the points above.

With that in mind, can you guess what a number of my stories will be about? Yup, you guessed it, sex and golf! I guarantee the golf stories will outnumber the sex stories, and that it will not be immoral like the story above. There will be a mix of stories, including some stories from my wife's and my travel and hobbies that we have turned to for distractions. Once again, this section will spare no details and will talk about things that may or have happened to you if you have the disease. This is your last chance to turn to the next chapter if you feel it hits too close to home. "Mom, Julie , Katie, Lauren," I am okay with sharing the details and even laughing about it as I tell the story, but I am sure that there is a psychologist out there somewhere that is trying to find my wife's phone number to have me put on some kind of watch list. I assure you I have been evaluated a number of times and they consider me sane and harmless.

TRIMIX

As I mentioned earlier, the plumbing started failing soon after I contracted the disease. It started by not being able to hold an erection without the aid of Viagra or Cialis, and it slowly got worse with time. After a while, neither Cialis nor Viagra could get the job done either. It was clearly time to take more drastic action. I contacted Dr. Uri, (name changed to protect the innocent) my urologist, about what do to next. He told me that he works with a local pharmacy, and they have a special blend that should do the trick. He said that it is not called for very often, and that I should call ahead to the pharmacy at least two days prior to make sure they would have it when I needed it. He said that I should book another appointment through his nurse, and make sure it is the first appointment in the morning and that I should pick up the special blend from the pharmacy before I arrived.

Well, that Tuesday morning couldn't get there fast enough for me. My appointment was at 8:30, and I was at the pharmacy bright and early at 8:00 a.m., which is when the first problem arose, as the pharmacy didn't open until 9:00 a.m. Dr. Uri's office is very strict about appointments. If you are 15 minutes late, chances are you will not be seen, and it will be a couple of weeks to reschedule. This couldn't be! I was tired of not holding up my end of the bargain. Luckily, one of the pharmacists came in early, and I followed him in the door, which prompted him to ask if I was the guy here for the TriMix. It must have been my poker face that gave me away. Anyway, I arrived at Dr Uri's office just in time to avoid the 15-minute penalty period and was quickly taken to the back office where Dr. Uri sat on a little stool, and with a smirk, he said, "Drop your pants, and let's make sure you know how to use this stuff and that you're not allergic to it."

I don't know why I hadn't thought of it before, but it was just then I figured out that he was about to use this stuff on me. I am glad I didn't have much time to think about it, because I am sure I would have been pretty anxious about it. As it was, Dr. Uri had other patients to tend to so I wasn't going to get much sympathy, especially from a time perspective. Next thing I remember, Dr. Uri is telling me to hold my penis in one hand and the syringe in the other. As I was catching up to the first set of commands, he was barking out the next sentence telling me that I wasn't going to have much luck with the current size of things. It was the middle of the winter in northern Michigan, the kind of climate that causes major shrinkage when you drive 40 minutes to get to your appointment. What he was basically telling me was to find a way to become more erect in order to move on. Now, I never have been into the self-pleasure thing, especially under the pressure of having to perform in front of another male, even though he was a doctor in a professional environment. Anyway, the next thing I knew, he was telling me to stick the needle into my penis and not to be shy about it or it might hurt more. Somewhere in the middle of all of that was a lesson in the anatomy of the penis and why these drugs were going to work. A key point to remember was that the syringe and the trimix had to go into the meatus section of the penis. Then Dr. Uri got my attention again when he grabbed me to inspect the injection point, and said, "It's working, pull your pants up and get out of here before it is too late!" It dawned on me as I watched it grow, unattended, what he was talking about. All I knew was that I was becoming very erect and had on a very thin pair of pants and still had to get through a hallway full of nurses and a lobby full of patients. I could not move fast enough to get to my car so I would not become the morning's entertainment.

So, there I sat in my car, fully erect, with no clue how long it was going to take things to go back to normal. Dr. Uri told me to pick up a box of <u>Pseudoephedrine</u> along with the TriMix, and that would be the antidote, if I ever needed it. I started to read the instructions, and guess what? Many Parkinson's patients take medications that are called MAO inhibitors. Well, the so-called antidote was not going to work. The non-medical antidotes include long walks and cold showers. I immediately reverted to Plan B and drove home to take a cold shower hoping not to get pulled over by the police for something stupid and have to deal with the situation of explaining myself to the county sheriff, especially if I was **dyskinetic.**

Status update - TriMix has become an integral part of our team. It continues to work very well. **Lessons Learned** includes:

➢ Your Doctor will give you a range of how much your injection should be. They will tell you to gradually increase your dosage until you are comfortable with the results. Take conservative steps as you try the different levels. Too big a jump may lead to a four-hour plus erection and a trip to the doctor's office. Just think of the ED commercials and their statement that an erection lasting more than 4 hours may be a rare, but serious, side effect. It may sound like a good idea to stretch it out to a four-hour love making session, but you may want to consider your current medical situation and whether you or your partner are up to it physically. Otherwise, the risk reward factor may not be as good as you think.

You and your partner need to talk about the use of this drug prior to the time you plan on using it. It can be an awkward situation pulling out a vial and needle in bed or in the bathroom just prior to making love. Depending on your and your partner's maturity level regarding sexual subjects, you may want to get her involved in the application process, especially if you have a serious tremor. It is very difficult to get the needle to the right place if you are experiencing coordination problems. If you miss, it doesn't work, and you have only added to your frustration.

TRIP TO CANCUN

We just returned from a trip to Cancun, Mexico where we spent nine days in paradise. By the way, this was my first trip to Mexico. I had always been told to avoid Mexico, because of the crime, corruption, bad water and lack of quality hotels. Well, I don't know where somebody formed that opinion, but it sure wasn't in Cancun. It is my new favorite place in the Caribbean region. We were extremely happy with every aspect of the trip with a couple of exceptions. These two scenarios were not unique to Cancun, but there are things that happen in the world every day, and until you have lived in the world of the handicapped you may not understand the severity, danger or fear that these situations can create. So chances are, you will break rule number 1 outlined earlier in the chapter, and when you do, log on and pay the fine.

There were four or five things that happened that are worth talking about here. Once again, the human nature card played its hand, and this time it gave us some excellent insight into how we, as a society, respond in general to things that are not normal by our definition. There is another situation that speaks to how large corporations handle handicap facilities and how they portray themselves to their customers. First of all, let me say that even attempting this trip was a risk on my part, but I have refused to let this disease beat me, and if I can't do the things I love then I will not be happy until I find a way to replace them. There are risks everywhere in life, and I did not consider the risks that we were about to take to be outside of acceptable guidelines. So, this trip got started when my brother won his sale's contest at work. It appeared that his wife was not going to be able to attend so he called to see if I wanted to join him instead. We had done this once before in Hawaii and had a good time, so a repeat of that vacation would have been a welcome distraction. Well, the next thing you know, Melanie and I had traded for a timeshare for the two days preceding the event. For the next four weeks, my brother and Melanie coordinated all the details of the trip, including changing the participants a few times. The time finally arrived for departure, and my nephew was the recipient of the free trip. Mel and I would meet them in Mexico and do a little family bonding.

The first story revolves around the airports. We departed from Traverse City, Michigan, flew to St Louis, Missouri and then to Dallas, Texas and finally on to Cancun. On our return trip, we flew from Cancun to Chicago to Traverse City. Now keep in mind that I was a very frequent traveler, and so I know my way around most airports and still have status with most of my travel partners. Problem number one raised its ugly head. I just heard that Chicago was named worst airport for on-time arrivals and departures. I would like to add worst handicap facilities, as well, especially when it comes to traveling on United's commuter services. The small planes and restrooms do not cater to the handicapped. The planes parking on the tarmac using stairs instead of jet bridges, and the second-thought nature of accessible loading and unloading of the planes is inexcusable in this day and age for one of the busiest airports in the world. Perhaps one of the hardest things to deal with in my particular case is that if the medications are working, I will appear and act almost completely normal for approximately 20 minutes every 3-5 hours. In fact, every 3-5 hours, I go from being wheelchair bound to almost my old self. Not only does this play with your psyche, but you should see the looks you get from fellow passengers when you arrive at the gate in a wheelchair, and then board looking normal and then require assistance to deplane. We actually flew with three other couples that I noticed all the way from St. Louis through Dallas and then on to Cancun. Then back again from Cancun to Chicago to Traverse City. In other words, they saw me transform at least three times and use the handicap facilities to get through customs and traverse the airports in wheelchairs. I could see it in one man's face that he didn't appreciate the scam I was running. I think he thought there might be something wrong, but he didn't quite have the nerve to say something.

The second area I would like to address is the lack of standards that are deployed across the large hotel chains. We tend to focus on Hilton's to try and concentrate our points. Our profile specifies handicap accessible, and yet two of the hotels we were attempting to use could not accommodate our needs. Ironically, we typically get the better and more consistently equipped rooms through Hilton's lower brand names, such as Hilton Garden Inn versus the Hilton Flagship hotels. I believe this to be because of when the hotels were constructed. Both law and priority changes of an aging population are forcing hotels to be more competitive in this area. **Lesson Learned** – We give Hilton Gardens our Handicap Hotel Award - in particular, the franchise in O'Fallon, Missouri. On the other side of the coin, we give the Hilton Hotel in Cancun, Mexico our Rubber Chicken Award for the hotel that least lived up to our expectations. This is for multiple reasons. The rooms that were billed as handicap accessible were not by most definitions. I will give them a point for having rails behind the toilets, but 20 points off for not having rails on either side of the toilet that you could use to stand up with and 10 points off for not having toilets of proper height. The shower also gets 20 points off for lack of handles and no detachable wand. The bellman staff gets full credit for having sufficient wheelchairs and getting us to the room.

Where the big problem arose was in the public restroom by the pool and restaurant bar. The handicap stall wasn't properly equipped, and unfortunately, I didn't notice before I sat down. This became a disaster. I was stuck and not strong enough to lift myself, and I had nothing to pull myself up with. At first I thought it quite funny, but after an hour, the comedic value wore off. Suddenly, I thought, I am in trouble! My legs were asleep due to the circulation being cut off from the way they were positioned on the toilet. I had been yelling for help for almost 20 minutes and was having problems with the language barrier. All I could think of was the quote my friend would use when he was a Navy Seal and in a dangerous situation. He would say, "How do you think the obituary will read on this one?" If he didn't like the sound of it, he wouldn't take the mission (lol - like he had a choice). I imagine that my obituary might read something like, "Unidentified

American found dead on toilet with pants down around his ankles." That was enough motivation for me to yell louder.

Finally, I got someone's attention. He knew enough English to know I needed help and went and got three lifeguards from the beach. Once again, there was a language barrier as I was trying to explain to them that my legs were asleep and that they would not support my weight until they woke up. They struggled to figure out what my problem was, and they didn't understand that my problem was that I couldn't get off the toilet! They asked very politely if I had been doing drugs or drinking. I do not know to this day what they thought my problem was, but it translated to "we can't move him until we get a wheel chair." Well, we finally got out of there and I was hoping the ordeal was over. Five minutes later, the hotel security manager showed up wanting me to file an accident report, which I was more than happy to do, especially if it meant the situation would be fixed so it wouldn't happen again. The hotel even sent up a cheese, fruit and cracker tray that evening. The only thing I am still upset about is that I do not know whether the hotel has rectified the situation and installed proper equipment to accommodate those in handicap situations. I have even pondered the idea of becoming a consultant for Hilton hotels doing ADA (Americans with Disabilities Act) compliance audits. One positive aspect of this experience is that Melanie and I learned to carry two-way radios to always keep in touch. She knew I was gone a long time and that it sometimes takes me long time in the bathroom, but it will alleviate the wondering if we have radios and can contact each other as the need arises for either of us.

The next thing we knew, my brother and his son, my nephew, arrived and got situated in their room. The next thing you know, my brother is being called home to deal with a situation. Once we got the okay from my brother's wife that my nephew could stay with us, we began to plot the rest of the week. This is relevant because my nephew had never been exposed to a disease like Parkinson's before, and the summer of 2008 he will be serving an internship with NBC. We began to talk about ways he could leverage his internship to advance the fight. It will be interesting to see if we can do anything with it. We also began to observe people and how they reacted to my situation without any understanding of the situation. People have very active imaginations as to what is causing my condition at any given time. Most people assume that I am either drunk, on drugs or have a mental condition. What's for sure is that until I get to sit and talk with someone and explain the situation, I am not treated with the same level of respect that I am accustomed to because of my physical appearance. I now let these situations play out until I decide whether or not to address it head on or simply file the results in the back of my mind to use at a later time. In the meantime, we continue to consider creative ways to collect research information and educate the public. The latest idea we are considering is to incorporate a survey section into our website that would allow those who have physical conditions, like me, that are clearly visible "some" of the time to gain more information and to provide feedback about their experience. On a grassroots level, we have considered making business cards to hand out to people to encourage them to visit our website and complete the survey.

POND DIVING

It is often said that you have nine lives and once you use them all, you die. Well, if this is true, I think I used one the other day. I have a small decorative pond in my back yard that is made of pieces of slate in a figure-eight shape with a cascading, two foot waterfall. With my current balance problems, I have learned to stay away from the edges of the pond. However, one day I was outside working in the backyard with my wife and a friend whom I occasionally hire to do the things that I can no longer do. That day we were turning the pond on after a long winter, and I decided that placing the filter six feet from the edge of the pond was a safe distance. WRONG! The phone rang, and it was my daughter, Katie, wanting to plan her trip north for summer break. As I bent over to lift the filter, my knee buckled and I lost my balance and began to fall forward. When I did, my foot hit the side of the hole where the filter was to go. One thing that I have learned about my condition is that when I am running low on medication or going through an off period, I will move very slowly - freezing almost solid at times. If something happens that creates an adrenaline rush, I can respond with normal speed. At any rate, one foot hit the side of the hole. I lunged forward toward the waterfall, and my other foot tried to stop my fall and landed on another piece of slate, which gave way and sent me lunging in another direction. Then my other foot came forward, once again stopping my fall on another piece of slate where I then somehow flipped head over heels and landed on my back in the middle of the pond! Miraculously, I was still holding the phone above the water level and had only two small scratches to show for it. Well, the grunts and large splash were enough to alert my wife and friend to my situation who quickly arrived to find me lying in a smelly pond on my back with me telling my daughter not to worry, that I was okay and I would call her back later once I got out of the pond and got cleaned up.

THE KINGSLEY CLUB

For those of you who are not familiar with the Kingsley Club, it is a gem hidden in the north of Michigan just outside of Traverse City near the small town of Kingsley. It is a private club that sits out in the middle of nowhere on an approximately 400-acre parcel. It was designed by Mike Devries in the Allister McKenzie style with strong local influence from both Ed Walker and Art Preston. It opened for play in 2000. I believe that *Golf Week* has it ranked #17 in its Modern Course Ranking. For me, the course is full of memories and holds the #1 ranking in my heart for golf courses and my family golf memories. It is not often that a place, much less a golf course, can mean so much to a family. To me, the club came along exactly at the right time in my life in that I had just gone through a divorce and needed a place to escape doing something I loved. A five-hour drive from my home in Wheaton, IL was far enough to "get away" and close enough to go there when I needed to for therapeutic reasons. In the last six years, it has been one of the centerpieces of many of family, business and personal memories. Once again, it is in the spotlight as a source of therapy. I'd like to share some of the stories from the experiences there.

MY NEW GOLF HANDICAP (FINALLY A LEGITIMATE EXCUSE)

I have had an excuse for my golf game since I started playing. I was self-taught and cemented a lot of muscle memory into my swing before I ran into anyone who could help identify the flaws. The good news, however, was that I could hit the ball a mile and occasionally I could predict the direction. I could usually putt until lights out, though geometry and local knowledge helped. However, you could take my irons away, except my 5, which I could pitch and run from 150 yards with great accuracy, and I wouldn't lose a stroke. I was what I heard my friend Dave refers to as a scooper. When I was diagnosed with Parkinson's, it had a profound effect on my game for many reasons. I should have known something was wrong well before my arm went bad, because in 2004 I was hitting the ball 300+ yards rather consistently off the tee, and with the fairway woods, I wasn't bad. In 2005, I thought I was going to have a breakout year, because I was planning a 100+ round year. Instead my average drive length was falling fast, and at best, I was hitting the ball 225 and that was off the hill on 17 near the end of the year. After my arm problems developed, I could barely swing the club. This is where my investment in the Kingsley Club and my friendship with Ed really came into play. Ed has been a true friend throughout this whole ordeal, and I owe him a tremendous debt of gratitude for his support, as well as all of you that have chimed in over the last two years, as Melanie and I fought our combined battles of Breast Cancer and Parkinson's. This is especially true when it comes to the staff. I have never met a finer group of professionals. Their concern and help over the years has been appreciated. Here are some of my stories about Parkinson's, golf and the Kingsley Club.

TRAINING THE NEXT GENERATION AND OUR FIRST GOLF LESSON

We have a real luxury at the club to have Dr. Gary Wiren join us for a couple of weeks every summer. I was talking to Gary one day about my desire to continue playing golf despite my new handicap. He thought that was a great idea and cautioned me not to get too upset with my new swing limitations and not to dwell on the old days, but rather, to focus on improving from this point forward and to be patient. My sister was in town, and I had asked Gary to give a lesson to my nephew, Matt, who was visiting from Denver, Colorado. At age 11, Matt is a concert quality pianist, and he was playing with me at the club that afternoon for the first time. I didn't dare try to give him a lesson on my own, especially since I was having a hard time holding a club at the time. This gave me the luxury of watching the master at work. He assumed that Matt had never had a lesson nor been given any instruction for a proper swing. All of which was true, and even better, it gave me a chance to observe as if I was just learning the game, as well. What Gary didn't know was that it was not only Matt's first lesson, but mine as well, as a retired Parkinson's victim! I watched for almost an hour as he went step by step through a proper swing pattern addressing everything from teeing the ball up, to weight transfer, to finishing style. He also addressed proper mental state when playing. Matt has no problem with confidence, and it his confidence seemed a natural transference from his musical accomplishments to gold, as he was absorbing the information from Gary and fast as Gary would deliver it. When they finished, Matt had a picture perfect swing for about an hour and was hitting the ball considerably better. He fully appreciated who Gary was and his stature in the golf world. We went out afterward and played nine holes. Matt played very well almost holing out on #9 from the ladies tee high up on the south tees. The minute he got home, he wrote Gary a thank you letter quoting sayings out of Gary's book, *"Golf is a Ball!"* Matt had found Gary's book in my basement library, unbeknownst to me, during the week he visited. At an earlier time, Gary had worked with me work on my swing. He had stopped to say hi, while our party played 17. He noticed I was struggling, and I explained what had happened. I told him that the current diagnosis was Parkinson's. At this time in the progression of my disease, I was having considerable strength and balance issues - so much so that my driver, which was once good for 300+, was at best 125 now. I was getting no weight transfer and no assistance from my wrists at all, and when I did get weight transfer, I would end up losing my balance almost falling over and barely catching myself before falling to the ground. A friend of mine suggested that I ask Ed to install attachable tethers at each tee to keep me from falling off the elevated tees. Gary very quickly picked up on that fact and asked if I had ever watched Gary Player swing a club. I said isn't he the guy who starts walking when he hits the ball. Gary laughed and said that it is more of an exercise on weight transfer, and he offered to help me turn my falling swing into a planned event. We worked on it for a while, and I am still trying to perfect it and make it a permanent part of my swing. I have been told that it is quite entertaining.

Later on that year I was playing the course with a friend of mine, and Gary was out visiting groups that he knew. We were approaching the 9th hole when he came up to our group and asked how my game was going. I responded that I had to continue to make adjustments to my game mentally and physically, as evidenced by the fact that I had a driver in my hand on a 135 yard par three. He asked me what I was going to do with that, since I would never be able to hold the green with a wood on that hole. Now #9 at Kingsley is one of the most challenging and unique par three's that you will ever find. I think at most, it plays 160 yards from one of the seven approaching tee boxes, and depending on the day, either plays south to north on one set and from west to east on the other. On one half of the green, it is steeply crowned, and on the other there is a large bowl surrounded by hills on one side and traps on the other. We were playing the west tees, and the flag was sitting conveniently at the very bottom of the bowl. Dan, the course superintendent, must have been in a generous mood that morning when he set the pins. Okay, enough set up, here is the rest of the story!

I told Gary that the driver was a necessity, because I would have to hit it over 125 to clear the steep ravine between us and the green, and the large driver face would ensure I hit the ball. I told him that I had no intention of trying to hold the green, and if I was lucky, I would end up in the fairway or better yet close to the trap just off the side of the green on the low side of the cup. This would set up my second shot with a wedge that I could then hit out of the sand at the hole, and if I missed the hole I had a second chance of the ball rolling up the hill and then coming back at the hole again.

Well, I hit my tee shot and finished my swing with my imitation of the Gary Player walk. I actually hit the green just past the pin. As Gary predicted, the ball lunged forward toward the back of the green, but the hill behind the hole slowed the momentum enough that it began to roll back toward the hole as if to go in, exactly like

I described my second shot would do. Unfortunately, it did not go in, but instead rolled next to the trap, as I had called originally, and Gary laughed. We walked back to the carts and headed to the green side bunker where I proceeded to pitch out of rough about two inches from the left side of the hole and up the back hill until the ball lost its momentum and came back down the hill and into the hole. Gary laughed again!

Honest officer, I am not drunk and I wasn't driving

The final story of this trip happened in St. Louis at my son's house near to where we are building our new home. We had just spent a long day with our builder's wife who was doubling as our interior designer. I had gone home a little sooner than Melanie, who drove the car home. Just before Mel left, we got a terrible ice storm that rendered her front windshield useless. Since our car has a mailbox seeking destruction feature, the next thing you know she has taken out the neighbor's mailbox. She parked across the street from the now totaled mailbox and came inside the house, since the neighbor was not yet home so she had no way of letting him know what had happened. The next thing we knew, there was a police officer at the door inquiring whose car was parked in the driveway. When she claimed it, he questioned her about the hit and run on the mailbox, which she explained to him and then went over to explain to the neighbor who had since gotten home. It was then I decided to make an appearance, unsuspecting of what I was about to unleash on myself.

I was a little dyskinetic that day and slurring my speech. Well, the minute the officer saw me stagger up to the side of the car, he decided that my wife was lying to cover up for me, and that I must have been the one driving the car drunk and he wasn't going to call it in until I sobered up. He was just about to cuff me and put me in the back of the car when my son, Mike, and my wife, Melanie, walked up and asked what he was doing. The next couple of comments proved to be very interesting in that human nature showed itself yet again. This time it shown in a police officer trained to observe signs of intoxication. The officer assumed that I was drunk and that my wife and son were covering for me so I would not get charged with a DUI. Further, he assumed that because my plates were from Michigan, I was going to be rude and obnoxious like all easterners. It took a couple of minutes for us to convince him that I was suffering from Parkinson's and had not been driving the car.

There were many lessons learned on this trip, and it was our first trip since my disease had progressed to the stage of needing an occasional wheelchair. **Lessons Learned** are as follows:

➢ Make sure that you understand the Hotel definition of a handicap accessible room and that it accommodates your situation.

➢ For International flights do not be shy in asking for wheelchair assistance in the big airports. It is too far to walk and too many lengthy lines in dealing with customs and immigration. The wheelchair assistant knows all of the shortcuts and can easily cut a half hour off your trip. Tip them well. If you don't get a wheelchair at the gate, you will have a hard time securing one, so don't leave the gate area without one.

➤ Human Nature will always find its way into the equation if you appear different then everyone else. Someone will always assume the worst of your behavior. Educate those around you about your condition, as it may save some aggravation for you and others in potential situations.

YOU JUST NEVER KNOW WHO YOU WILL MEET ON A PLANE!

I just got off the plane were I sat next to a gentlemen and his wife. I leaned over to apologize in advance for the terrible singing that they were about to hear for the next hour and a half. My vocal cord problem was acting up, and I was feeling particularly self-conscious, since I had cleared out a section of the restaurant at lunch the day before at the Red Robin with my singing and the blank stare that takes over my face when I am in off mode. I could not help it, and later I went up to apologize to the manager if I had cost him any business, and as well to teach him and his wait staff a lesson on life. You see, the week before I was in there and had the same waitress. I had pulled her aside and told her what my problem was and told her that if there were any complaints that they should feel free to come talk to me, and we would figure out how to fix the problem.

Well, everything went fine the first week. This time, however, when I walked in I stumbled as I climbed into the booth, as they tried to seat us first. That is all it took to convince the hostess that I was intoxicated, and she tried to discreetly get the manager not realizing that I could pretty much read her lips, as she told him what had happened. The result was a threesome of managers showing up at the table next to me to observe my actions and find a reason to throw me out or call the police if I acted up. They sat there for almost an hour and even had the store manager come out and ask them how I was behaving to which they replied, "He is behaving now except for the noise." The store manager left avoiding eye contact as he walked by. About the time we were finishing, there was a shift change, and they started seating people in our section again. Since we were done, I decided not to put another group through my singing. I sought out the manager and pulled him aside. The waitress in the next section who was doing all of the complaining earlier ran up to hear the conversation. Well, I think I caught him off guard when I showed up behind him and asked if he had any clue as to what was going on at lunch. He said his staff had told him that I had a drinking problem, and he had his managers come watch me in case I got out of hand. I apologized if I cost him any business, but since I was writing this book, I had to see how far it would play out before someone asked me if there was a problem they could help with or if old human nature would win out again. Guess what? He then apologized and said he would explain the situation to his staff as a lesson. I told him that I would personally bring him a signed copy of the book.

So when I got on the plane, my previous experience with negative human nature had gotten the best of me, and I assumed the people sitting next to me on the plane would behave the same way. Boy, was I wrong. It turns out that the guy was a doctor who was fascinated with my case and even took the time to read the book for the rest of the flight. I gave him a copy of the book, as he has some experience with the Botox procedure that I am contemplating, and we are scheduled to talk sometime next week. There is hope!

BE PREPARED!

I knew my Boy Scout experiences would find their way into this story somewhere! The good thing about Parkinson's is that it typically moves slowly enough to allow you to prepare for the next stage. Bad news is that it tends to lull you into a false sense of security. It appeared early on in my case that loss of balance and physical strength were going to eventually have a major effect on me. In addition, the problems going on with my vocal cords would become an issue, as well as bowel and bladder issues. The least of my problems was that if I kept losing weight, I would eventually have to buy a new wardrobe. Last, if I could not get around by myself, I would need assistance 24/7 and probably a new vehicle to get around in. This is a pretty daunting list, especially if you have already looked ahead and reviewed the outline for finding the right people and keeping up with the paperwork, but they are all subjects that will have to be addressed, and the sooner you do it the more opportunities you will have to pick them off when it is convenient, as opposed to when you have to.

Our first step was to review our home to see what it would take to make it ADA (Americans with Disabilities Act) compliant. We hired an architect and contacted a friend who was a builder to talk about what we needed to do. We also took the opportunity to add a couple of features that we always wanted. This was an eye opening experience in that the cost to remodel added to the value of our home from when initially purchased, but our costs to remodel were going to exceed what we could ever sell our house for. This, combined with a very tough winter in Michigan and the birth of twin grandkids, enticed us to look at relocation to St. Louis and building a new ADA compliant home. Talk about scope creep! We have been so focused on the kids and the new house, in addition to the regular trips to the various doctors, that we have not had much time for the rest of the list. This became a problem this week when I was walking into a store, and my jeans practically ended up around my ankles. So, we made an emergency shopping trip to buy new shorts and pants to get by. I am hoping that we don't get invited to any formal events, because I will be swimming in any of my suits. Since it is summer, I can get by with very little until my weight loss stabilizes.

We started looking at new vehicles to replace the ones coming up on lease expirations although I currently do not require a wheelchair I do not travel very well in the front passenger seat of most new cars. This was costing us time and money in that I could not take more then 3-4 hours in a car on a given day. We began test driving all of the crossover vehicles and SUV's. Gas mileage was a consideration but number one on the list was would it pass the "butt test." Meaning, could I stand to sit on the seat for more then 3-4 hours per day? Other considerations high on the list included:

- ➢ Did the wife like it, since she would be doing 100% of the driving
- ➢ The "butt test"
- ➢ Large enough to handle at least three grandchildren in car seats
- ➢ Gas mileage
- ➢ Affordability
- ➢ Enough storage capacity to handle a fold-up wheelchair at some point and golf clubs for now
- ➢ People comfort features

We test drove over 12 vehicles including Lexus, Cadillac, Mercedes, Nissan, Saturn and the typical cast of players. We decided by an overwhelming margin that the Buick Enclave was the best car for our current situation. It blew away the competition in every category except price. Buick is pretty proud of their product, as they should be, and they are pricing it accordingly. The support for this pricing level comes also from the fact that it is the #1 selling car in its class, and there is a shortage of them due to the GM supplier strike. I am happy to report that we have one trip on the books to Detroit that we made in record time, and all was well.

NEW HOME

We began construction on our house in St. Louis in March hoping that it would be finished just prior to the winter season setting back in. We were also trying to take advantage of low interest rates and a flat housing market. This worked to our advantage in a big way in St. Louis. We told the builder up front that we were not in a hurry to move out of northern Michigan to St. Louis in the middle of July or August. In fact, we considered keeping our home in Michigan so that it would be available to us during the summer season. Our home in Michigan is up for sale with not much action. The market is depressed everywhere without exception. We knew going into this thing that getting stuck with two houses for a period of time was a real possibility, and we have done some planning to accommodate that possibility. We have a number of single friends that would make good house mates in Michigan, and we hope to find some in Missouri, as well. We will make them an offer they cannot refuse if they will live in our house like a roommate paying their share of the expenses. This works especially well if they happen to be a nurse, as well, and we can leverage their skills in the event of an emergency. We built our new house big enough so that the kids would always have a nice and somewhat private place to stay if they were down visiting, or if we got to the point of having live in help, we could still accommodate everyone nicely.

Other things we are planning for include:

- Wills and trusts
- The funeral ceremony
- Friend phone lists
- The facilities
- Organ donations

> ➤ Alternate planning horizons should I be cured or Melanie be stricken with something

VOCAL CORDS

My vocal cords have a condition called Strider. In my case, my right vocal cord is paralyzed, and my left one is partially paralyzed. The problem this causes is that as they progressively come together, it will begin to affect my breathing and my eating, meaning that eventually I will have to have a tracheotomy or I will not be able to properly breathe. In fact, I might be getting pretty close to that point now. This is one of those landmark days with this disease in my opinion, because it makes your condition known 24/7, and you now open your body up to all kinds of new possibilities for disease or infection, not to mention that you could lose your ability to speak under the wrong set of circumstances. With this entire situation in mind, this is the one procedure I think I fear the most, and it is probably why I have been procrastinating on it the longest. There may be an alternative to this process using, of all things, Botox. In this procedure, they use the Botox to deaden one of the vocal cords in a very strategic place, which stops that cord from having dyskinetic options. This surgery was developed to treat dyskinetic vocal cords or a disease outside of the Parkinson's family, but I am told it is sometimes used in the treatment of my problem. Let the great debate begin! The vote is 3-3 within my immediate circle of doctors, and the ones for it are just more adamant that it will work than those that say it won't. If it does work, it is only a short-term fix, because the BOTOX will wear off in 2-3 months, and then we do it again and hopefully it works again. What I am trying to do for the first procedure if I can get it approved is to have both the ENT and the Botox doctor in the room at the same time so if something goes wrong, we can quickly switch over to the tracheotomy procedure before there is any damage done. The problem is that the two people I need to make this work are on opposite sides of the solution and are four states apart physically. Well this I am told by both sets of doctors is not a plan that is going to work.

HIRE THE RIGHT PEOPLE

You are not going to believe the number of people that are about to touch your life and then present you a bill. If you are in a private doctor's setting, this number can be controlled, but once in the hospital, you have no control. The biggest problem that this creates is that too many of them are administering drugs to you, and as usual, the more people that are in involved, the more complex it becomes and the problem is not only drugs but the recordkeeping is a nightmare. Well, it appears that help is on the way arriving in a couple of different forms. Many hospitals and centers of expertise are moving toward Customer Centric Models, and systems and staff catch up. Well, Mark Bosche, Inc. is a Customer Centric Model, which means that we not only look at the medical aspect of things, but we also integrate that information into the budget, personnel and communications with family and friends. It needs to transcend the competitive barriers that exist between the people you are hiring who may be from separate competitive vendors, or something even simpler like a doctor's ego, which I define as the all inclusive way they run their practice.

Do they have the staff and procedures in place to support the collaborative model that will be required to run your project? It is important that we keep on top of the research and development (R&D) projects that are going on in this area. The benefit of having your information complete, accurate and timely, and transportable in an easily portable manner is key to anything you do. So pay attention to how you might be able to collect your information from each doctor you are about to hire.

INTERFACING WITH THE DOCTORS' AND FACILITIES' EGO (SYSTEMS)

Now, here is where my career comes into play. I have had a number of projects that have allowed me to build some expertise in how hospital systems work or don't. My years at EDS were running large accounts, like Oldsmobile Customer Service and a large business and organizational reorganization project associated with a company called Neodata, among others. One of my early jobs, while I was in school, was working as an operation's person on weekends and holidays at a local hospital. I parlayed this into a job with a local software company, which got parlayed into running the sales and operation's organizations of a company called A/R Mediquest. It was an early attempt at a unified information system for hospitals, so I got a lesson on how to create a Customer Centric System. At EMC, I was the business development manager for all of the internet projects going on in North Carolina, and I got involved with a couple of Customer Centric Model projects. Okay, enough of a history lesson.

Here is how this is relevant. One of the things you potentially need is an integrated database that combines all information from all entities that you deal with. Most of the systems out there stop at the walls of the providers. So your challenge is getting this information to the central database. The question is where will that be housed? Who owns it? How is it paid for? Now that you have this vast mountain of information, the questions arise about who can use it for analyzing trends, cures and symptoms for research benefiting the big race? Here is where human nature rears its ugly head again. The lack of trust for how people will use confidential information about you or against you has added considerable time, cost and complexity to solving this problem. So, therefore, there are multiple entities working on solving the same type of problem. In some countries, the government is taking charge of the project and will police and monitor it. Companies, like Web MD, will try a commercialized version in the U.S. and abroad with the sales mantra of you own your data no matter what your employment situation or who your insurance carrier is. Your local hospitals and places like Mayo are spending huge sums of money creating Customer Centric Environments. So with all of this going on what do you do?

I would suggest for now that you explore what is available to you and at what level the information exists. I found that I have informational mountains at Mayo in their database format, Munson Medical in their database format, and an EMC (Web MD solution) site with their format, not including all of the traditional paper-based systems that exist in the doctors' offices that are outside the networks. Next, understand what that system can do for you. Can it give you adequate documentation so you can provide it to new doctors and tell them the story. If the answer is no, then get yourself a big three ring binder and start collecting every piece of paper you can get your hands on. Design a system for pulling information from your files that is disciplined enough not to give away your originals. I wish I would have done this when I first started having problems. I am afraid a lot of very valuable information has been lost over the last two years. Let me amend that statement. I am sure that every piece of paper that was created by the doctors' offices still exists. The real question is how you would ever go back and assemble it? This method will not only allow you to keep copies of all the documents but will provide you with an accurate sequence of events should you ever need it, which you probably will! If you are lucky enough to have a system capable of collecting all of this information, I would do the following:

➢ Monitor it to make sure all sources of information are finding the way there.

➢ Understand who has ownership of the data and if there are limitations on its use, for instance. Will EMC allow me to access this system when I am no longer an employee receiving insurance coverage? If the answer is no then this system will do you little good in the long run if it forces you to change midstream.

➢ Understand if the system has import and export capabilities and who they are set up to deal with.

➢ Understand what you have to do to get copies of the data. Is there an online system available to the patient? Is there a doctors' only section?

➢ Remember there is a new statement to replace "He who has the gold rules!" It is, "He who owns the information rules, because he knows how!"

➢ Get a copy of a standardized Medical Information Release Form, and get it on file for each provider you are dealing with.

After writing this chapter, I decided that the letter I had been meaning to send to Jack Mollen, senior VP of Human Resources at EMC, was long overdue. I sent the letter, and he called me back a short time later offering his help in any way I needed it for this project. Since then, I have been working with his staff to figure out how this chapter should be written. By this I mean, since Jack was named Human Resources Manager of the year by his peers in the industry a couple of years ago, I should have known that his long-term plans would have included ways to deal with most of the problems described in this book. That decides it, I can't be sick yet. The systems needed to obtain the information to develop a cure are not yet available, and so we have to call this thing off until they are! Good thought anyway. Back to the three-ring binder and the systems that are partially in place. This will be material for the "find a distraction" section.

UNDERSTANDING YOUR ORGANIZATIONAL CHART

You are impacting a number of people with your disease from friends, family, coworkers, doctors, lawyers and you will even touch people you know nothing about when you sit near them at dinner in a restaurant. Each of them will have a different way they will want you to deal with them. Based on their role in your life, you may need to be direct or indirect in your methods. The following chapters talk about how to deal with various situations based on some of the experiences I've had during my Parkinson's period. Once I finish the book and get the web site up and running, I would like to set up a section of the site dedicated to these subjects and I would invite anyone who has observed or been directly involved with someone with Parkinson's tell us about their experiences. I will treat this like a blog or community site where people will be able to share their perceptions, opinions and/or experiences. There will also be experts available on our website to answer questions you may have.

HIRING AND FIRING AUTHORITY

This is an important area in, in that you need to surround yourself with people who can positively affect your situation. You must quickly assess what each has to offer and whether or not you want them to be a part of your team and begin documenting their part in your story. I believe some grassroots wisdom applies here, such as the following:

➢ Be upfront and direct with the people you need. Tell them what you want, when you want it and how you want it to look, as well as the budget you're working within. Share with them your plan and accept their input and hold them accountable to it.

- ➤ Treat them as if they were an employee of great value contributing to the success of your company. Offer immediate praise and feedback. Pay your bills on time if that is your relationship.

- ➤ Twenty percent of your people will take 80% of you - learn their idiosyncrasies and play to them; it will save you time and headaches.

- ➤ If required, put them on a performance plan.

- ➤ Fire or demote them appropriately within your hierarchy of importance or replace them if you feel there is someone more qualified for the job. Remember, most of these people are here to help you out of the kindness of their hearts, so treat them accordingly. However, a negative attitude can have an effect on your whole team. So move fast if you have to, and be direct about it.

- ➤ Communicate early and often - there are too many moving pieces not to.

THE INTERVIEW PROCESS

Whether it is a formal or informal process, this is an important part of your selection process. I like to ask people questions about themselves first. In this way, way you can hear about what they think of themselves, as opposed to what they think you want to hear based on knowing your goals and objectives. Have a plan for each interview. Understand the following:

> ➢ Is this a forced marriage? In other words, are they your only option, and if so find out their idiosyncrasies so you can deal with them most effectively.

> ➢ Find out who they think their competition is and ask them to rank their competitors. Nobody knows better than a competitor who the best is. Understand why they think that. Ask them if they were in your shoes what would they do? Would they hire themselves? Why should or shouldn't you hire them?

> ➢ Understand what problem they can solve.

In my case, since I live out in the middle of nowhere, a pretty nice nowhere by the way, I need to often travel to see experts on my condition. I have had to develop a team of local talent and secure other team members in distant locations. Knowing this up front gave me additional questions to ask during the interview, like how well they play with other children and if they shared their toys when they were a kid. You need to make sure you are getting a team player or else it will destroy the effectiveness of it.

I see about a half dozen neurologists. I have had to deal with each having their strengths and weaknesses and learn what their role is on the team. For example, I have a local neurologist, one at Mayo, one at Frasier Rehab, one at NIH and soon one in St. Louis.

YOUR DOCTORS

Dr. Bruining is my local neurologist. We have a very good relationship. We had a conversation early on about what her strengths are and where we might want to seek additional help. She fully understands the insurance and paperwork processes associated with a long-term illness and knows how to write the letters required for approval. She has a great office team, and she has privileges at the local hospital, which come in handy should you ever end up there. She coordinates the communication with other physicians when appropriate and takes the lead on telling how to play on the team. She has great bedside manner for me and my family and knows at which level to communicate the message. She will act as the historian for paperwork and my medical history when necessary to get newer doctors up to speed when my condition changes. She has been very responsive to ideas that me or my wife have had regarding the treatment process. I truly feel that I am not a patient, but rather, part of a team that just happens to be focused on me. What she will readily admit is that she is far away from the centers for research and is not set up to handle studies very well but would cooperate if there was one that could fit within the limitations of the area, i.e., recommending the best facilities and specialists in the area. Dr. Bruining serves the most important role a doctor can play on my team, and that is local doctor, overall project manager and confidant.

IF NINE OUT OF TEN DOCTORS AGREE, FIND THE 10TH AND MAKE SURE YOU UNDERSTAND WHY!

Dr. Litvan plays more of a consultant role. She has a strong research and discovery background. Most importantly, she knows the definitions, early warning signs of symptoms and progression definitions of most movement disorder diseases better than anyone else I have found. That includes experiences with the Mayo Clinic and Rush Hospital Chicago, The National Institute of Health and miscellaneous other medical institutions. All pretty big names and egos, so I am sure I will hear from some of them as to why I am making these comments.

Well, first of all, let me say that my opinion is very subjective, and I am sure that someone has a formal process to evaluate the effectiveness of a doctor. The first question I would ask is what is their perspective? Are they a hospital administrator who's going to evaluate with a bias toward patient profitability, or are they a nurse who is going to evaluate you by how you write orders? My working diagnosis at the time was PSP. This was first diagnosed by Dr. X at Mayo Clinic. I remember him telling his students that my eyes were not tracking the way they were supposed to so that is why he thought I had PSP, and so my working diagnosis for almost 6 months was PSP. Other doctors saw Dr. X at Mayo Clinic and fell into the trap of it must be correct if nine out of ten doctors agree, especially if they are from the Mayo Clinic. So for six months, I proceeded down the path of educating myself and those involved with my case on PSP. In fact, I was flown out to the National Institute of Health (NIH) all expenses paid to see the experts there and document my case. They keep a national database on a variety of diseases and have to validate your condition before they can refer you for a study. They fell into the same trap of assuming the previous diagnosis was correct and referred me to Dr. Litvan, who was conducting a study on PSP. It coincidently was one that we had just found on our own through the internet, so we already had an application in. Knowing we were blessed by NIH, things seemed to flow a little faster.

Dr. Litvan had her research assistant respond back to our email, and we were invited down for an interview to participate in the study. We drove down to Louisville, Kentucky from Traverse City, Michigan, which was about an eleven hour drive to our first appointment. It was scheduled for October 20, 2007, at 2:30 p.m., and she showed up about a half an hour late due to the fact that she was reviewing my file, and by looking at the notes and a copy of the MRI, she was able to determine that I did not have PSP and would not be eligible for her study. Initially, I was shocked. How could this be? Nine out of ten doctors agreed! I think it was a result of that misdiagnosis that I decided to include this section and what to title it.

Dr. Litvan eventually did a physical evaluation. She then sent me home to have some additional tests run, and she told me to return in March after the disease had progressed so it would further defined itself. I returned in March a little sicker and a lot more defined. I was taking Parcopa (Sinemet) in a 25/250 configuration about every three hours. I felt like I needed them every 2 ½ hours, but my body could not take the side effects. This time, I was scheduled at 2:30 p.m., and we saw her at 4:00 p.m. This time she was late because she wanted to take care of some things so she could spend more time with me. At this point in my progression, I was running an on/off cycle every three hours, which means that my body was burning through a 25/250 tablet of Parcopa every cycle. When I was "on" you could barely see the effects of the disease. The problem was that this only lasted for about 20 minutes. When I was "off" I often needed a wheelchair to go down a hallway, and this off period would last for approximately a half an hour. The rest of the time, I was somewhere in between. The only saving grace was that I could predict, with great accuracy, when I would be on or off based on when I took my medicine and what time of day it was. I also got early warning signs of when the switch was about to be thrown. When I was about to shutdown, the left side of my mouth would start to pull, the left side of my neck would tense up to where it would eventually start to pull across my shoulder, my left arm would start to go into protective mode and my left foot would start to curl in. When I was about to turn on, my inner left ear felt like there was a bug crawling in it about two minutes prior.

Well, Dr. Litvan now had all night to observe my symptoms, and she spent about three hours with my wife and me watching me through a complete cycle to see for herself if my story was true. There we sat running all of the dexterity tests that we all know and love associated with Parkinson's so we would have a baseline to determine where my off periods were taking me. Suddenly, I got my warning itch. I had told Dr. Litvan earlier that I would give her a signal, and she should stand up and wave her magic wand or wiggle her nose or whatever her favorite witch command was for executing a spell that would cure me for the next twenty minutes. She didn't play along until I got up from the chair, where I had been stuck for the last ½ hour frozen solid, and walked down the hallway as if nothing was wrong. We even recorded it on videotape for historical purposes.

96

We then talked about how we might change my medications to prolong my "on" periods and stop my freezing episodes, which are yet another problem. She prescribed some new medications for me to try at home, and I picked them up at the pharmacy immediately upon return. We tried the first one and had some dosing problems with it. The first night on it, I was having hallucinations - it was the *War of the Worlds* all over again. We scheduled a follow-up inpatient therapy session for the next month at the Frazier Rehab Clinic in Louisville, Kentucky. I believe they are ranked the #4 rehab clinic the U.S., and they may be underrated. I was to spend a week there initially, so I scheduled a roundtrip flight to St. Louis to work on the house. We arrived Monday morning and were met by Dr. Litvan's staff for an orientation of the hospital. We also were introduced to the nurses and told of the procedures that we were to follow. Frazier Rehab is situated next to both the Children's Hospital and Barnes Jewish Hospital and shares some facilities with each. The facilities were nice but not out of the ordinary for a top notch facility. We soon found that the rule we would always apply to hospitals, which was to bring our own supply of medication and medical supplies applied here as well, much to our nurses' chagrin. The hospital standard for catheters was the cheap, red, rubber kind, and I had a bad history with that variety and asked them to find the ones that I was accustomed to. They were accommodating, but it took two days to find the first two and four days to find the remainder of a case. Luckily, and thanks to my wife, we had enough to get by. Another issue we ran into was obtaining the right formulation of Sinemet or Parcopa. We ended up using our own there as well. I have found that being a

Parkinson patient in a hospital requires a special attitude by both the patient and the nursing staff, and as usual, I was the anomaly.

Since we were experimenting with new drugs, I had a number of pills that were scheduled on request or based on effectiveness and current dosages and whether the dosage required a change in time administered and frequency and mix of the various medications I was taking the day before. This doesn't fit any of the nursing procedures, so my wife and I spent the entire visit trying to keep the peace with the nursing staff. We were keeping our own records on the drugs I was taking as well as keeping an event log of how I was reacting to the various medications. My wife and I fully understood how the nursing staff was operating, and one by one, I think we got our point across. Since we were pretty self-sufficient, I think the word got out to leave us alone unless we called for assistance.

The first night on the new drugs was an amazing success. I slept through the night for the first time in over a year until a lab tech burst through the door at 4:30 a.m. to give me a blood test - so much for the sleep experiment. A big sign went up the next day which read, "Do not disturb between 11 p.m. and 9 a.m." We spent the next couple of days fine tuning the dosing and frequency of the drugs under the supervision of Dr. Houghton who was filling in for Dr. Litvan who had left to attend a seminar in San Diego. This was kind of a bummer, because I would have liked to spend more time with Dr. Litvan discussing some other subjects. However, Dr. Houghton was great to work with as well, and he got on board with our program to break out of jail early, as we called it. We had accomplished what we set out to do and needed to get to St. Louis to deal with some issues with Patty with a "Y." This meant an early discharge on a weekend. In all seriousness, the nursing staff was great and very conscientious. They clearly had the patients' best interests in mind in everything they did, and a weekend checkout was a big inconvenience for everyone involved, since the PT and OT staff had gone home for the weekend and not written their final reports, but they pulled together as a team and made it happen.

With the early departure, we also did not get to say goodbye and thanks to the physical and occupational therapy nurses. As I mentioned earlier, I think this team is underrated. Their attitude and bed side manner was great, and they did a great job of adapting their exercise programs to the various patients that were in the center. They made it fun! It was here I came up with the idea we should make golf a part of the physical therapy programs nationally, and I would love to work with their staff to institutionalize it. Maybe we can do it at Valhalla CC if they decide to support the legendary Golf Club Charity Event Series being proposed.

YOUR CARE FACILITY

I have also found that if there are numerous tests which need to be performed, it may be worth going to the Mayo Clinic to minimize the time it takes to get to a final answer. Mayo is a lot better equipped than Traverse City is to handle a bunch of tests in a short period of time. You may also find that overall, they may even be a little cheaper because they probably participate with all of your insurance companies and you don't end up paying out of pocket costs, such as out of network fees, and you receive reduced co-pays. For single tests or reoccurring lab work, our local hospital works just fine. You should search long and hard for physical therapy facilities. Your equipment needs will change over the course of your treatment, and you need to make sure they can change with you. Finally, you must consider what you will do if you reach the point where you can no longer be left alone. If there is not sufficient family around, you may need to consider a group home or assisted living care facility.

> **Palliative Care Providers** – Talk to Dr. Fraser or Patricia Hoban at Munson Medical Center in Traverse City, Michigan

> **Caregivers** - We have employed a series of different solutions as it pertains to caregivers, but for the moment, my wife is with me 24/7. With our pending move to St. Louis, we will be back in the market looking for at least a part-time care provider. Currently, we can get by with a minimal skill companion because of my balance and stability issues. Our homes in St. Louis and Interlochen are both big enough to allow a live-in caretaker scenario should we ever need it. Once again, I am lucky that I have the financial means and family support to handle just about every situation, and so our experience here has been limited thus far. The one time we did hire a temporary nurse, we got one who had let her licensure expire, but she was also a certified massage therapist. This worked out well on some days. She has since

reacquired her nursing license, and my wife was able to get her a full-time job at the hospital with benefits.

➢ **Lesson Learned** – When seeking a nurse or caregiver, seek a match based on both technical capabilities as well as how flexible they are about what they are willing to do. If things continue the way they are, we may need the person to help edit newsletters or books or to pitch in on one of the projects we have in development. With me running the ideas by both a new person and Melanie, who knows how this could work out. What I need now is to find ways to monetize some of the pilot activities I have started. There is no one out there more anxious then me to be able to return my social security check for a while. If the project that we are proposing to the President as I write this chapter comes to fruition, there should be enough work and budget to hire an aide that is capable of helping out on some other fronts as well. We have also talked about better leveraging our support groups' talents in both St. Louis and Traverse City. There is a lot of talent there currently sitting idle. By combining efforts, we could be reducing our daily living expenses and working toward the goals of the project. This would make a good rehabilitation project to get some of these guys back into the workforce and offer a valuable support service over the phone or internet. I know the individuals involved with the Traverse City YOPD Group, and I will be contacting the group in St. Charles, Missouri shortly to find out their interest in any kind of projects.

FINANCIAL PLAN

Note: The information contained in this section is only my experience, and should not be misconstrued as legal advice from an expert. This should be treated as a tool to provide some direction toward figuring out a financial plan. Your first phone call should be to your attorney to begin the process.

In this section, I will share with you how we set a financial plan in place and what we learned through the process and what we might have done differently. So, if you go into your financial planner and ask him about your planning horizons, he may wonder what planet you are from, since this is a concept that I developed for my particular situation. I am sure that other people use something very similar and call it something else. The key point here is make sure you have someone you trust, and who can get along with your spouse and/or your executor. Keep on top of this, and treat it like a working document. As fast as your life changes, so will your financial picture. One of the biggest worries since all of this has happened has been that after my divorce, I did not have or make enough time to reconfigure my plan. So now I am stuck in this endless debate on how to get the kids the inheritance that I would like them to have verses having enough cash to let Melanie live out her life comfortably after I am gone. Distractions like these life changes happen to all of us, and if it's not a divorce, it could be something else - a job change, loss of a loved one, etc. My point is to encourage you to find a good financial planner, tell him/her your goals and insure that they take charge of keeping your plans up to date based on the changes in circumstances in your life.

INSURANCE AGENT

Your insurance agent will play a key role in your final plans. Hopefully you had the foresight to load up on life insurance and health care coverage prior to discovering your illness. There are a couple of things that you may want to talk to your agent about sooner than later, such as how your life insurance policies are going to payout. Some policies allow you to cash out up to 50% of the cash value of your policy if a doctor will certify that you have a terminal illness and you have less than six months to live. If this is an option, you might wish to consider it. If it is not an option, then you may want to consider naming the beneficiaries directly in the policy. This way, once the claim is filed and processed, a payment will go out immediately to the people you name in the policy. If you run it through your trust, you may add months to when your loved ones actually see any benefits from your policy. The other thing that I did with my estate was to buy an additional life insurance policy for my wife to insure that she has enough to support her for the rest of her life and that my kids, too, will receive an inheritance.

YOUR BOSS

In my case, my boss and his entire management chain were unbelievable. He knew more about Parkinson's than I did when I was first diagnosed and he knew what to expect. They worked around my schedule until I was forced to retire because of the progression, and they did an excellent job of getting my paperwork approved in a timely fashion once we made the decision and understood the critical nature of the timing. The decision for me to retire was a difficult one, as I was having too much fun working, and I had a number of key client deals set up to close in some very nice places in Europe.

Since my wife had been managing my travel arrangements working with my company's travel agent, Corporate Travel, we would often travel together when I got sick in case anything went wrong. With all of the frequent flier miles I had earned through my travel the last two years, we didn't have to pay for much. Both Burney and Tim deserve a "Manager of the Year" award for the way they handled my case, and I will always be indebted to them. Having been in their shoes, I can appreciate what they endured. First of all to lose one of your top number-producing salesmen in the middle of a major sales campaign is a challenge. They also know that if I had the chance to come back, I would, and so they kept my position open for a while just in case. They also rearranged my workload to make sure nothing fell through the cracks. I also must thank Gareth, Marco, Beth and anyone else who pitched in to help. The guy who probably got the brunt of the work, however, and probably was least appreciated for the work he did was Glenn. Without him, a number of things would have fallen apart. Once I had retired, Burney basically implemented the Mack truck plan and told everyone not to call me so I could keep my priority on my health. We made trips to talk to key customers to inform them what was going on and let them know how this would affect their piece of the business. We both assured the customers that although I was retiring, I would not be far if there was an emergency. To this day, we remain friends and talk occasionally and update each other on goings on. One of the first things that I was taught in manager's training at EDS was to know your people. This is key to a successful organization. It is just as important that you, as an employee, know your boss and understand their ability and clout in the organization to get things done. I have always told my kids that when they take a new job, the first thing they need to do is assess their boss and put him/her into one of three categories, which are:

➤ **The flyer -** This is a boss who will not be in his position very long, as he has been placed there for strategic reasons, and once he is done with his mission, he will be off to something new.

➤ **The incompetent -** This is also a boss that will not be in his role for very long either, but for the wrong reasons.

➤ **The Peter Principle –** This is one who has reached their maximum potential within the organization, whether deserved or not, and they will probably go "no hire" and they know it.

I have had all three types, and I have learned the hard way the advantages and disadvantages of each. My advice is to find and work for a flyer and have a frank discussion with him/her about what your role will be in the progression/succession plan and stake your claim. I hadn't thought about how critical having this kind of boss could be to an employee in a situation like mine. They are able to pick up the phone and make things happen very quickly for you, if needed. Both Burney and Tim fit this description.

In the case of the incompetent manager, you need to have a meeting with their boss and understand what the management chain thinks about him/her. If the manager is clueless about the situation, get out of there as fast as you can. You don't want to deal with this situation. They will not do a good job of promoting you by word of mouth through the organization, and even if they do, who would listen? If they do promote you, you will be tied to the failure of your team when they finally figure out what is going on. If their manager knows there is a problem, then once again stake your claim if that is what interests you. Chances are, they don't have a replacement or they would already be gone. Start doing as much of their job as possible and make yourself the obvious choice and clearly delineate yourself from their management organization to be sure that you are not part of the problem. Once again, it is important not to get caught here either, because if they can't do their job right now, how will they do in processing your situation when the time comes? If you get stuck in this situation when you are afflicted then make sure you have a Plan B. This would probably work best if it included your Human Resources group or you sought out a manager in the organization who you would consider a flyer and beg for an adoption while you go through the process.

In the case of the Peter Principle boss, you may want to consider the same Plan B. There is a number of things that I have seen go wrong in these organizations. The first one is that these types of managers are always looking for the easy way out. Your leaving is not going to be the easy way. Therefore, if it is beneficial for you to go, it may not happen at the pace you need it to. The other issue you may run into is that these types of organizations usually have some sort of problem going on. Once you show your vulnerability, you become the perfect scapegoat. This is a problem in that you will not be around to defend yourself, and your reputation could be at stake. This is a real problem if you need to someday come back to work. You know, like when we find the cure for this damn disease!

YOUR FRIENDS AND NEIGHBORS

Next to your spouse and caregiver, these people are your biggest assets for endless reasons, as in my case. You will quickly find out who is really your friend, because they will often step forward offering anything they can to help. We have so many people to thank here that I don't know where to start. The best advice I have here is to be upfront with your friends and neighbors, and keep them informed as to what is going on. They will often know better then you what you need, especially when it comes to moral support for both you and your family. Remember, the patient isn't necessarily the most affected person in this situation. Once you're gone, they are the ones left to deal with your loss and your affairs. This is clearly the most difficult situation for a spouse to deal with and often their greatest fear in life. These are the people you will need to count on to help your family through the process. This is especially true in my situation, and I m still trying to figure out how to deal with it most effectively. The problems that we are dealing with are many, and I would suggest that you look at our situation for similarities and try to deal with them while you can.

For instance, we are moving to St. Louis to be closer to family and expert medical care. We love Traverse City and have some of our best friends are real close by, we are about to put a 700-mile gap in our relationships. This is not the first time that both Melanie and I have had to deal with a situation like this. We both relocated shortly after our divorces and lost the support network we had built in the Chicago area. We managed to hang on to many of the relationships, but they are definitely not as tight as they used to be. We anticipate making new friends to be a little harder with the illness being involved, but we are very optimistic about our prospects, due to the fact that there are very large Parkinson's support groups in neighboring towns and the fact that we have so much family there, which is where I need to be spending my time. However, until I am comfortable that someone is St. Louis is going to be capable emotionally to step in for Mel, I intend to have a code word with her best friend, Pat, and if I use that code word, she is to jump on the first available flight or train or start driving at my expense and get down here.

Since we have not sold our house yet, we are concerned over what kind of absentee neighbors we will be. Financially, we can handle the two payments for a while, but would definitely find better ways to spend the money other than double house payments, and we continue to work a Plan A and a Plan B. We had someone go through the house this week who appeared interested. He is looking to retire and move back up here from North Carolina and get away from the 100 degree heat. I have heard that our house is being considered in his top three, so let the full court press begin.

YOUR HUMAN RESOURCES GROUP

Your Human Resources group will be one of the most important contacts and resources to develop, especially if your company has policies similar to EMC. I would encourage you to take a couple of hours to sit down with someone who understands what your company has to offer and how it applies to your situation. This will be key in the development of your financial and medical plans. It is also important that you keep in touch with them over the years, in case anything changes. The HR department at EMC has been great to work with. So much so in fact that I sent a letter to Jack Mollen thanking them for all their assistance. I also mentioned that I was writing this book, and he expressed his interest in being a part of the project. I do not know where this will take me, but I do know that Jack is well-respected throughout the industry as being an innovator and understanding where things are going from an industry perspective. As I mentioned before, it seems that Jack and his staff have a plan for most of the problems I have outlined in this book. This is a **Lesson Learned** for me in that if I would have gotten a hold of Jack or some of the senior members of his staff a little sooner, I may have been able to better utilize some of the things they have been working on with WebMD at least in a beta mode.

Your trainer

Your physical health is important; if you are currently using a personal trainer, continue. If you are not, than it might be a good time to find one as your muscles get weaken by not being used and if you have someone prodding you along it will help you stamina and your well being.

Find a support group

Here is that human nature thing again. People like to hang with people most like them, right? Good luck with that one! Parkinson's is non-discriminatory in who it strikes, although it seems to favor men over women and older people vs. younger, though it appears there is a growing number of patients across all demographics. I believe that what is important here is that you need to find a group of people who are living your world. It will assist in more ways than imaginable. We joined the Grand Traverse Area Parkinson's Foundation Young Onset group. We picked this one as it was in close proximity to our home. Since joining, we have both advanced our working knowledge of Parkinson's, as well as having met new lifelong friends. We usually meet once a month officially, and we attend an annual summer forum that packs the house. The priority on this exercise should be high. We learned more about Parkinson's, its definition, its normal progression, the secrets of dealing with the local Social Security Administration, the local medical scene, home remedies, and most importantly, we met dozens of new friends whom we have become very close to. I would suggest a couple of things while you search out a group right for you:

➤ Find out what you can do to add to the experience of the group. Just because you're newly diagnosed doesn't mean you can't add value. I have found that what you lack in history will be made up for in energy.

➤ Find a group that does not support a monthly pity party atmosphere.

➤ Explore both the on-line and local forums - join both and share information.

> ➢ Become a part of the group - a silent observer doesn't do anybody any good. Carve out your niche. Lead, follow or get out of the way!

> ➢ Find a group that supports both the patients, as well as your caregiver.

> ➢ See if you can find a community-supported group. They tend to be tightly tied to funding sources and community resources you may need.

I would also like to take this opportunity to recognize the efforts of Maxine Meach and Catherine Shovan who have work so hard in putting together the Traverse City group. Their vision and foresight has been invaluable.

START WORKING ON YOUR PHD

This would require me to finish my bachelor's degree first, but in life experience, I am probably working on my second or third degree. One in business, political science, child development, creative financing, construction management and farming would be the minimal that I could probably qualify for.

COME OUT OF THE CLOSET AT THE RIGHT TIME

The old saying, "Your whole life flashes before you" was a fairly accurate description of what happened to me. I was overwhelmed by the thoughts rushing through my mind - most of them related to how this was going to impact my family. Once again, I was somewhat lucky in that I was hundreds of miles away from most of my support systems, so I had to physically pick up the phone and call them to tell them what was going on. This also gave me some time to think about who to call first and what to say. I would suggest that one of the first people you call is your Human Resources specialist for several reasons. First, they will be able to explain to you your benefit level and inform you of potential concerns. I will guarantee you that both your spouse and your boss will want to know the results of that call in the first two minutes of your conversation with them. You might as well beat them to the punch. The second reason is to allow you some time to tell the story in your head a couple times when it doesn't count as much. Third, it is a layer of protection in case someone tries to do something stupid regarding your job. I have heard some urban legends of some cases where a boss found out he might lose an employee to a serious illness so he put the employee on the layoff list, because it was eventually going to happen anyway. Your Human Resources group can help in these areas.

I always believe that bad news doesn't get any better with age and travels at the speed of light relative to good news traveling at the speed of sound, which leads me to a couple of points for you to consider. Tell people know sooner than later and make sure they find out from you and not through the rumor mill. In most cases, they would prefer to hear from you and would like the opportunity to ask you questions. The second point is that you need to adopt a philosophy of how you are going to deal with your information and decide whether you are going to give the whole truth and nothing but the truth or whether you are going to have an abbreviated PG rated version. We have opted for the whole truth and nothing but the truth. You may also prefer a mixed message to deal with immature audiences.

PRIVACY AND MODESTY - GET OVER IT!

As you have seen, this disease can cause a lot of embarrassing situations if you let it. Believe me you will maintain your sanity far better the sooner you put modesty aside for the sake of medicine. I got over it during what I refer to as my Blue Man Group Audition at the Mayo clinic.

It was during my first trip to Mayo, and Dr. X wanted to see how much of my autonomic system was being affected by the disease from a diagnostic standpoint and also to establish a baseline perspective. So, he ordered what I refer to as the Blue Man Test. For this test, I went to the lab in the Neurology Department, and they give me a key to the dressing room and a hospital gown and told me not to worry about getting it all tied up, because I would not be needing it for the test. I was to then go the waiting room when I was ready, which I did, and I waited and waited. Finally, a nurse appeared, and she apologized for running late and asked if I was ready. She then explained the procedure to me, and she took me into the preparation room where another nurse told me to strip down and lay flat on my back on a cold metal table. They then told me they were going to proceed to cover me with a salt-like substance that is orange in color. They said they needed to make sure that every square inch of my body was covered, and then they would put me in a thermally controlled room for approximately 45 minutes or so. They asked that I lie perfectly still so I would not knock off any of the salt-like substance. I was still on the part where these two nice looking, young nurses were going to strip me down and rub every square inch of my body!

They finished applying the substance, and they then rolled the table I was on into the thermally controlled room. It looked like those easy bake ovens that our sisters had when we were kids. Then a voice came over the speakers asking what type of music I wanted to listen to that was most likely to keep me still. The 45 minutes seemed like forever. Next thing I knew, I was beginning to turn blue in little spots all over my body. I asked, "What is this about?" They explained that the blue spots indicated where I was beginning to sweat. She said that they would take a picture every time they turned up the heat so they could determine where I was most sensitive to heat. Well, guess what turned blue first?

This went on for a while, and about every 10 minutes, they would have me pose for a picture, which involved making sure that I had a wash cloth over my private areas. I could only laugh at the situation. That was until I had to use the bathroom, and I mean I had to use it! At first, I decided to try and hold it until the nurse said, "Is there something wrong?" I explained my situation, and she proceeded to tell me that if I got out of the oven then we would probably have to start over, and they would not be able to do it again that day. I asked how much longer, and she said at least 25 minutes, and I replied that that was not an option. They said, it's too bad that you do not know how to use a catheter, and I told them that I had just graduated from the catheter 101 class in Urology the previous evening. What timing! Next thing I knew, I had a catheter and a urinal, and thus, we were able to finish the test!

When I was finally blue all over they told me that I was done and wheeled me out to the dressing room. I think I spent over 40 minutes in the shower trying to get all of the blue salt-like stuff off of me. It was everywhere. I went to dinner later that evening, and my waitress asked if I was an actor or something. I laughed and said, "Why would you ask?" She said the only time she had seen someone that was that blue was in Chicago, and they were an actor who had just finished show. Okay, I know you are dying to know what turned blue first. The arm pits! I asked for the pictures to prove it, but they would not give them up.

GET YOUR ACT TOGETHER

When Michael J. Fox was campaigning for stem cell reform, he was criticized by Rush Limbaugh for using his medications or lack thereof to help make his point. Bad move on Rush's part to pick on a public icon, especially on the subject of his affliction. Rush should have known better, even if he might have been half right. You will soon learn as a patient or a caregiver that most of us will succumb to some sort of "on/off" cycle that is usually triggered by when we take our medications or other events, such as eating a protein rich meal or exercising. Everyone is a little different. I seem to be in an every three-hour cycle at the present, and thanks to Dr. House and her staff at Frazier Rehab, my down periods are less intense and shorter in duration. However, make no mistake about it, they are still there. You need to look at your schedule and compare it to your cycle once you figure it out. You need to decide what you can do when you or on and what you can do when your off. In fact, I usually ask my neurologist whether they want me to

115

be off or on the next time they see me. By understanding your cycle and how it impacts your abilities, it will allow you to reduce your frustration levels. You can do a better job of setting expectation levels with friends and loved ones when you understand your on/off cycles.

You should also decide how you want to deal with adversity. I am to the point with my vocal cords where I cannot eat without making a lot of noise. This is not a problem with those that know what is going on, but it can be quite distracting to others in a restaurant or on an airplane. We have cleaned out a whole section at a restaurant before, so in fairness to my poor waiter or waitress, I try to pull them aside and explain what is going on and tell them that they are free to share the information with anyone that asks about me. I also tell them to have people feel free to ask me directly if they have any questions. One of the things I decided early on is that my new job is that of an educator, and I will take any opportunity that presents itself to do my job. I have also printed up business cards that I will begin to hand out to people when my website is done. I use these when the situation looks like it could get out of hand, or I am shutdown or short on time.

The **Lesson Learned** here is that people are usually very understanding and even compassionate when they understand your dilemma. Get the word out as soon as possible, and you will improve everyone's experience. Once I get this book finished, I intend to carry around a signed copy that I can hand to people when their curiosity results in a conversation. You would be surprised how many people I strike up a conversation with who tell me they have a friend or loved one that they have been curious about for years, but they have either been afraid to ask, or the person was unwilling to share.

ADOPT A CAUSE DEAR PRESIDENT BUSH, SENATOR OBAMA, SENATOR MCCAIN

The deeper I get into this subject, the more frustrated I become on a number of fronts. The good news is that Parkinson's is truly recognized as one of the more expensive diseases out there from a healthcare and human toll perspective, and there is a lot of money being spent on finding the cure thanks in part to the efforts of the high profile individuals that have gone public, such as Michael J. Fox and Mohammed Ali.

The frustrating part is that there are so many people and organizations being formed to address their particular piece of the puzzle that we become locked in bureaucracy trying to sort out the priorities, especially now that stem cell research shows such promise, and Washington has decided to make it a political decision. I tried to make this an issue for the 2008 presidential election and even tried to get a debate focused on it to take place in Traverse City as a part of the National Cherry Festival, but the idea came too late in the game, and at the same time, gas prices hit over $4.25 per gallon. I am attaching the letter that I tried to send to each of the candidates, as well as President Bush. At this time, I do not expect to hear anything else from either party. I still believe that it is the right thing to do, and I still intend to pursue a solution one piece at a time. So, I went to bed thinking about this, which is

117

always a problem for me, because I end up thinking about it all night until I either figure it out or sit up in bed out of frustration and wake my wife up, as well. Well, this particular night was a "solve it" night. It created enough ideas and concepts to keep me busy for a lifetime. I call the document that I produced the next morning the "Dream Document." Of course, the date I had dreamt this would occur, July 4, 2008, has passed. However, I would still like to share the dream with you, and the ideas associated with it, which includes a letter I sent to President Bush and Senator Debi Stabenow. The dream is presented below.

- George W. calls a press conference on 7/4/2008 to announce he is putting out the challenge to find a cure for Parkinson's.
- Goal Demonstrate that Corporate America can join with government and research organizations to find a cure for Parkinson's. Set the example for a prototype National Health Fund Raising Program for a specific disease.

- Find a Cure for Parkinson's through established channels and leverage projects that show the greatest promise. Do it in a way that Kennedy challenged us to be the first to land on the moon.
- Have George W. Bush announce the pilot program and have George senior and Bill Clinton announce their intention to be the honorary chairs of a non-partisan group.
- Leverage Traverse City Cherry Festival.
- Governor Granholm announces the formation of new Michigan Company that has been formed to deal with the resulting entity required to administer all of this.

➢ McCain and Obama have their first debate on health care here to find ways of creating private/public partnerships to develop cures for the most costly diseases that exist.

➢ Assemble the existing organizations plus a new one www.parkinsonMSAsupport.com, which is a rarer but more aggressive form of Parkinson's. The goal here is to find the cure before it takes anyone on this stage, or they will die trying.

➢ The speech would take place on a stage at the shores of Lake Michigan during the Traverse City Cherry Festival on July 4th and would be held in conjunction with a debate between Senator Obama and Senator McCain with the subject being National Health Care System Plans followed by an exclusive fund raiser or thank you dinner for the day at a place in Traverse City.

The following people will be in attendance:

One or both of the Presidential Candidates, John McCain and Barack Obama, will be present in support of the project, and it will be non partisan, because it will make the fundraising easier and cut the political red tape out of it that none of us, literally or figuratively, has time for. High profile patients and advocates like Janet Reno and her husband, Michael J. Fox and his wife, Muhammad Ali and his daughter, Mark Bosche and wife Melanie (it was our idea) and the Blue Angels Flight Team (as they are already scheduled to be there) will adopt this as their cause until a cure is found. It will take a waiver of the DOD rule against the Angels sponsoring any organization. I would ask that you make a call to get a waiver for the sake of the marketing program associated with making this self-funding. They will form an alliance with the private golf clubs around the world and produce a golf tour and a marketing program around the series. This will be a non-profit organization that will help pull together the history books of each club and will work with the Blue Angels, so that their golf schedule follows the Blue Angels.

One of the fundraising ideas is a celebrity golf outing to coincide with events on CBS or the Golf Channel and Rollout of the Story Teller Series. Donald Trump agrees to run an apprentice-type show in support of the cause. Each week, the elite golf courses of the world challenge each other to a fundraising contest, and he who has the most money wins. Each week there are two one-hour shows. The first show will introduce the clubs featured, and the next week the results of the competition from the week before will be shown.

Proposed idea: The first week will be a challenge between the Kingsley Club and Whispering Pines in a golf tournament sponsored by the Kingsley Club. The Kingsley Club will be playing for the democrats and the Whispering Pines guys will play for the republicans. Each club will recruit their own stars and will be allowed to acquire them any way they so choose. The public will call in and pledge money to the team they want to win. The winning team is the one that raises the most money. In addition, each hole will be worth a skin. A company will be allowed to sponsor the skin for a minimum dollar amount. Events will be private at these clubs except at designated locations, so that the courses are not damaged and less money needs to be spent on security and other miscellaneous expenses. Besides, most clubs will not support the crowds. Only club members and event-sponsored staff will be allowed on the course that day.

The following letter was sent to the president's office on June 25, 2008, via email. It was rejected as being too long. I sent another shortened version the next day as a teaser to get the bigger plan in the door. It too was rejected, and I was told that the White House does not have time to read it, and I was politely told to do the work and follow the political processes in place - no short cuts. I also sent a copy to Debi Stabenow's office, and they actually read it and got back to me to tell me that they liked the idea and to let them know how it progresses. Since the guy that read it was a federal employee, he could not legally share it with any political candidate. It figures - the one guy that offers to help and actually has the drive to get it done has been neutered by the political process. This is why they call it bureaucracy! The letter I sent reads, as follows:

Dear President Bush:

Seldom does a day come along that affords us the opportunity to solve so many problems with a string of events that could play out by leveraging what are now uncorrelated events demanding tremendous amounts of energy, creativity, personal sacrifice and government resources, as well as taxing local, state, federal, corporate America and charitable organizations. The opportunity I speak of would allow for combined resources to be channeled into the success of a new project that could have major implications in solving issues of public health care funding, finding a cure for Parkinson's and setting in place the process toward finding cures for other diseases. This could be achieved by creating a sustainable project, which could be the legacy of your administration in the area of creating bonds between private and public charitable organizations and medical research, as well as saving the lives or improving the quality of life of tens of thousands of Americans and millions more around the world. The cause is finding a cure for Parkinson's. The date is the Fourth of July, 2008, and the place is Traverse City, Michigan. Please allow me the opportunity to answer the questions this has undoubtedly raised in your mind already before I explain what I am asking you to do. First, I would like to provide a little background.

I suffer from a progressive form of Parkinson's called MSA or Multiple Systems Atrophy. It is a progressive and aggressive form of Parkinson's in the family of diseases. I am one of the luckier victims so far when it comes to visible conditions, but it has had devastating effects on my internal systems. I have been declared totally disabled by both the Social Security Administration and the Hartford Insurance Group. I am lucky in that to date I have had the funding to carry me to this point by the generous personnel policies of the EMC Corporation and some advanced planning on my part on the insurance side of things. I am also lucky in that I have had a supportive family throughout this ordeal. My wife, Melanie, has left her job to be able to care for me 24/7. Again, I am fortunate to still have the strength and the mental capacity to begin to share my experiences with the world on how to cope with Parkinson's and/or other terminal illnesses, and I am writing a book about the experience. In the book, I make some recommendations on how a person can manage their personal health care activities as if they were the CEO of their own health care entity, as well as empowering them to make decisions for their life based upon educating themselves about their situation.

I realize this book will not be for everyone, as it involves some pretty complex issues, and I am sure I will gain my share of critics, but I feel that I am bringing a fresh message to the victims of Parkinson's, and the information I will provide will be generic enough to apply to all afflicted with a terminal illness. I have decided that I have taken the concepts far enough, and that I would now like to find a couple of people who would be willing to focus their research on this subject in acquiring their PhD, as well as seeking other organizations or projects focused on education to help finish the project. Besides, I need to make sure that this is not all lost as my illness progresses. I am not looking at retaining all the rights to the ideas expressed here, as it is too important to get greedy over.

What I do need to make sure of, however, is that I put a revenue stream in place in case the Social Security Administration decides that I am employable and this boils over to my LTD insurance company, for this would be devastating. I would need to quickly replace a considerable amount a month in income due to the fact that I am selling my house in Michigan and moving to St. Louis, Missouri to be closer to family. However, due to the economy in Michigan, I have not yet sold my home, and my home in St. Louis will not be completed until July 31, 2008. I have been working on this book whenever I have a free moment, and I rely on my wife considerably for her typing skills and some editing. I am fortunate in that I have found some doctors that can treat some of the symptoms to give me a better quality of life. Despite not being able to urinate without the help of a catheter or pass waste without the process of an enema or make love to my wife without the aid of an ED drug, I feel fortunate that I can still swing a golf club, and with the aid of a cart and the patience of a few friends and the facilities of the Kingsley Club near Traverse City, I can still play a few holes of golf.

I then shared the dream, as I have shown above, and I supplied my name and contact information for any questions they may have had. I have already shared the outcome with you, which came in the form of polite rejection and instruction to follow proper protocol in such matters.

UNDERSTAND WHEN YOU GET A "DO OVER"

Understand when you get a "do over" because Parkinson's can effect so many systems, and it tends to (in my case, anyway) change symptoms almost as much as I change shoes. You have to be very careful about decisions that you make and the long-term impact. Anytime a doctor makes a recommendation to me, I have a number of questions that I immediately ask. Regarding medications, I ask: Will this interfere with any of the medications that I am currently taking? What needs to happen for me that will allow me to stop taking this drug? Does it preclude me from taking something else? What are the known side effects? What are the chances of me reacting to the known side effects? One of the most important questions I ask regarding medications and any procedures that are recommended is: "If I take this drug or have this procedure done, what will it eliminate me from doing in the future?"

Many of the early Parkinson's medications simply wash through your system with little or no serious side effects. Sinemet, which has been the gold standard for years, has a half-life of three and half hours with the usual side effects being constipation or dyskinesia when over or under dosing. I then began taking a class of drugs known as MAO A and B inhibitors, which tended to work very well at stopping certain symptoms. I also started on a drug called Azilect for a while, and it worked very well. At the time, I was on a three-hour cycle, which meant I would go from fully functional to bed ridden every three hours. When I first began taking Azilect, most of my down or off time subsided. It was a new wonder drug for me. Then I started to notice some things, like when I would eat certain foods, I would get physically sick. If I missed a dose, I would get in trouble too quickly. I needed to have a procedure performed, and I couldn't use a pain killer during the surgery. The cold medicine that I would typically use warned against using with MAO inhibitors so finally I decided to quit taking it. Even when I decided to get off the drug and try something else, it took two weeks to wind down from the dose I was on, two more weeks to purge it from my system and then another several weeks to get the dosing right on the new drug. In the spirit of this chapter, I got a "do over" so I took the chance.

Now, let's talk about some cases that haven't gone as well. I have met a large number of fellow Parkinson's patients that have had the disease for almost 20 years. Some of them have had procedures done within the brain to help ease the pain caused by dyskinesia. Pallidotomy and thalamotomy were some of the early procedures performed. They worked by removing a part of the brain that was causing the problem. This is an example of a "no do over." Once you have done it, there is no chance of ever curing that part of the brain, because it is gone. I think that is why I am so hesitant to have a tracheotomy performed, because deep down inside, I know that this may be one of those no do over decisions I may need to make to stay alive so I can keep hoping for a miracle. Every once in a while, I will get relief from my breathing problem for a day or two, and then the problem returns. Maybe just one of these times, it won't. So, I guess Lesson Learned here is that sometimes you have to go one for one to be successful instead of four for ten. You just need to figure out when.

STAY ACTIVE PHYSICALLY AND MENTALLY

One of the biggest mistakes people make is to allow their body to shut them down both physically and mentally. It happens very easily due to the fact that when you perform any type of physical activity you burn dopamine, and the more you burn, the worse you feel, not to mention that since you are getting less exercise overall, your muscles will be reminding you of how hard you worked the next day. Do not get dragged into this downward spiral. In fact, while I was doing inpatient rehab at Frasier, I was able to work through a down period without taking medication. This is a phenomenon that I cannot explain any other way than that my body kicked in and produced some extra dopamine.

It is just as important that you stay mentally alert, as well, because your brain, like your muscles, requires work to stay finely tuned. In fact, I have found that I need to be twice as sharp as I used to be to offset some of the negative impressions people form about me based on my physical condition, not to mention that I usually have half the time to get something done, because of my physical condition. If will be helpful to you if you can involve others in keeping you physically fit. We have some equipment in our basement that I can work out on, but I do not dare use it without a spotter. We also have many neighbors that walk every day for exercise, and we are always welcome to join in.

I also enrolled in a water ballet class at a local spa and health club for a while. One day I was talking to my neighbor, Liz, and she told me of the water aerobics class she was taking every Tuesday and Thursday mornings. It sounded like just what the doctor had ordered, and so the next day she picked me up and off we went. Well, once we got there, I found myself in a pool amidst 20 women who probably ranged in age from 50-93, but in their hearts, they were 20. I quickly acclimated to the rules and regulations of the group and proceeded to get my butt kicked by the instructor and the ladies who had been doing these routines for years. The water is a great place to exercise, but there are also things that you need to watch out for, including working out in water that is too cold, because it can cause you to freeze up and do more harm than good.

Be careful in the facility if you have balance and stability issues, as the floor around the pool is always slippery making it very easy to fall. Finally, your ability to regain your stance in the water may have diminished over the years so make sure you have a spotter in the pool, as well. Of course, there is always golf, which I will always find a way to play - I don't care how sick I am. I was joking with a fellow golf addict of mine who has advanced stages of brain cancer and has had a significant portion of his brain removed due to the cancer. He has used golf to keep his sanity and as physical therapy to help retrain his body how to function on at least three occasions that I know of. I said, Ralph, I've got to tell you of my current state of affairs. I told him that my disease had progressed to the point where I couldn't piss without a straw, I couldn't crap without a pill and an enema, I couldn't make love to my wife without a syringe full of medication, I couldn't drive a car much anymore and I would fall frequently, but I could still play nine holes occasionally when I was having a good day, even if I had to use my driver on the par threes. Life is still very much worth living. His response was, "Has the Parkinson's affected your ability to count your strokes all these years, as well?"

KEEPING UP WITH THE PAPERWORK

This section is aimed at sharing with you my experiences as they pertain to handling the processes and emotions around these critical and emotionally-charged subjects. It is not intended to be a "how to" manual or an attempt to replace or reduce the costs of working with trained legal professionals that you either have or will have in place. If you would like further information on how to contact some of the professionals that we have used, please go to our web site www.parkinsonsMSA.com. The next section is devoted to addressing all the paperwork it takes to run your life again. Each person is a little different so pick and choose the variety you need.

UNDERSTANDING YOUR WISHES

There are many ways legally, spiritually, emotionally, financially and even comically that you can make your wishes known for when you are gone. The more well thought out and complete your documentation is, the more you can rest assured that your wishes will be carried out. The following documents we will be addressing can be filled out for many different reasons. Usually, they are completed out of love, but also for reasons as simple as saving time and money in avoiding probate court, avoiding taxes, donating organs or other important assets, getting the last word in a friendship, revenge, cleansing your conscience or making sure sentimental things end up where you want them. In any case, you need to take each of these documents and think through your strategy on how they should be used. This strategy could be very simple or very complex depending on your financial situation and/or family life.

I recently got together with a number of my close friends that I have known since high school, and I brought my son along in case I had some medical issues that arose that I needed help with. My wife usually helps me with these kinds of things, but this was to be a guy's weekend. My son, Jon, happened to be free that weekend and flew in from Chicago with my good friend Tim. We had originally planned a weekend of golf and would stay at the Kingsley Club's member cabins for the weekend. These cabins are perfect for these kinds of things. They are four bedrooms each with two queen size beds, a full bath and more than ample desk space and shelving. In addition, there is a screened-in porch overlooking the 17th hole that may soon be one of the most talked about holes of golf in the state. The cabins also have a kitchen and adequate storage area for your golf bags. There were eight of us at peak times, and everything cooperated except the weather. Now, the word close doesn't necessarily imply that I have seen them recently, and the weather being cold and rainy may have been a blessing in that it only allowed us to play about three holes a day for the three days we were there. Instead, we sat around and reminisced about old times, old girl friends, old sport's stories, early career stories, our kids, our families and about everything else that can happen over 30 years with a group of good friends. We talked until the wee hours of the morning. I was not included after about 11:00 p.m., or I would have paid for it the next day by being completely immobile due to the Parkinson's. What I was able to do was to hear some of the conversations that were going on with my son Jon. They were my friend's versions of the stories of my life. Suddenly, I was inspired to start writing out of fear that my legacy would be told by Dave Champion, and who knew how that might come out! It was then I started to write the last chapter for that weekend and will be able to have the last word at the right time.

FIVE WISHES

Most states have something called Five Wishes, this let's your family and hospital staff know your wishes before the time comes to make those tough decisions. There is also Living Will or a durable power of attorney, this replaces those forms. Five Wishes takes away any advance directive you had before.

A LIVING WILL

The Living Will is important so that people understand how you want to live or not when the disease or whatever ails you progresses to a certain point. Some of us are able to deal with this conversation, while others are more sensitive about it. However, it is important that your family, friends and/or legal counsel, and most importantly, your medical care providers understand your last wishes. A split second decision may determine whether or not your wishes are followed, and if not made by someone in the know, you may not get your wish. This could result in additional pain and suffering for you and your family, as well as accumulate additional medical costs. It could also cost someone their life in the case of a person who would like to be an organ donor, and the organs cannot be harvested in time for a waiting and needing recipient. What may be most important if the situation arises is that you are telling your family that it is okay to let you go when the time comes, and they have to make a decision. This document is pretty standardized, but you should see an attorney to get it drafted to make sure that the rules within your state or country of residence are followed. They will also be able to walk you through the various scenarios that they have seen and discuss how you want them handled. This should be a relatively inexpensive process. If you do not have the money to hire an attorney there are software packages online that can be used if need be, but I would use caution and make sure that you go over it with your wife, family or executor if they are not one in the same.

TRUSTS

Here is where you can learn the most from my mistakes, so I encourage you to read and follow closely. A trust is an instrument that can do a number of things for you. It is typically used to set up a financial plan that provides for your heirs after you are gone. It is also an instrument that can protect your assets from taxation and people who may have different plans for your estate than you do. The trust laws vary from state to state and are subject to many IRS rulings on what you can or cannot do. They are also controlled by the marital laws of your state, and there are also many inheritance laws that come into play as well.

Probably the most important aspect of the trust is how it takes care of your heirs, thus, further defining your legacy. This has been the most complex, emotional and time-consuming aspect of my estate planning. This is for multiple reasons based on family and my financial situation. Due to the complexity of my personal situation, i.e., being divorced and remarried, and having six kids, four from my former marriage, and two step children with my current wife, Melanie, and the fact that Melanie and I have only been married for a little over 4 years at time of writing this book. We had taken a number of estate planning steps, but clearly, were not ready for the double dose of bad news we got back in 2006 with her breast cancer and my Parkinson's. This news not only put my estate plan into the spotlight with my family, but also halted the ability to make any significant changes to my financial situation. If you are reading this book because you are a victim, you are probably in the same position and looking for similar alternatives. Well, after about six attempts to get this document in a condition that satisfies my wife, my kids, my ex-wife and my attorneys, I decided, at the suggestion of my two sons, to hire a professional estate planning consultant to get the benefit of their experience and to get an unbiased opinion of my plans. My daughter-in-law is an accountant who works for a relatively small accounting firm in St. Louis called Brown, Smith and Wallace. Within this group, David Heilich is the Practice Leader of the Family Wealth Planning Group. David has more than 14 years of experience, and he is responsible for the growth and development of the Family Wealth Planning Practice. This practice serves family businesses, wealthy families and executives with comprehensive wealth management services. David's areas of expertise include:

- Estate Planning
- Family Business Consulting
- Income Tax Consulting
- Advanced Planning
- Financial Planning
- Family Office Services
- Estate and Trust Compliance

David also provides expertise on various individual, partnership, estate, gift and trust income tax related issues to the tax and accounting services group. Prior to joining Brown, Smith and

Wallace, David served as a Tax Manager and Director of Estate and Trust Services at MPP&W, P.C. In addition to his consulting and compliance responsibilities, he also was primarily responsible for all aspects of providing services to a prominent St. Louis family office. He is a licensed certified public accountant and a member of the American Institute of Certified Public Accountants, the Missouri Society of Certified Public Accountants and the Estate Planning Council. David earned a Bachelor of Science Business Administration degree in accounting from St. Louis University. Once again, I have one way of evaluating someone like this. It is also very subjective. Does this guy get the job done, and am I happy with the results? This is clearly not my area of expertise, and the mistake I made was not to find someone like him earlier. Instead, I tried to get by using a common sense wisdom method to get this done. This was a mistake, and I am lucky it didn't backfire on me by having something happen before I got it corrected causing further grief and frustration over my estate. I had a lot of legal experience over my life and have seen a number of things play out similar to this, and so I over estimated my abilities to overcome these shortcomings and didn't place enough value on a consultant to help me through the family issues that were before me. Dave was very upfront and candid with me about the documents that I had produced to date. I felt like I had just gone through a red pen review of a business proposal at EDS. This was often compared to having a frontal lobotomy by most managers. I have never had a frontal lobotomy, but I understand that it is a very painful process. At any rate, I was so impressed with his thoroughness, attention to detail and his ability to hear what I was saying were my priorities and translating them to the document that I have asked him to help me explore ways to exploit his services and make them available to people who read this book or use the associated services that I hope will spring out of it. Stay tuned to our website and look to see if we are able to put something together. You will find us at www.parkinsonsMSAsupport.com.

POWER OF ATTORNEY

Power of Attorney is a document that essentially transfers your authority to someone else when you are gone or incapacitated. Obviously, if this is the case, you need to make sure it is someone you can trust. You also may want to consider having separate legal documents and designated individuals to have authority over your medical needs or financial needs. This allows you to choose an individual that may have more experience in such matters or someone with whom you have discussed your wishes with in detail and are confident they will honor them. This person is key to being able to execute your final wishes when the time comes.

FINANCIAL PLAN

We talked this one to death in earlier chapters. If you chose to go through the exercise, make sure that your plans are part of your personnel file folder and that they are in sync with your other documents.

BENEFICIARY FORMS

Beneficiary forms should exist and be updated for any financial asset that may pass to your estate or members of it.

CONTACT SHEETS

The contact sheets are also very important in that if there is a change in your medical status, this will be a tremendous help for people who need it. Contact forms come in all shapes and sizes, as many different people use them for many different things. I would go grab a folder and label it "Important Papers - Look Here First." Make sure that these forms are kept up to date, and that they contain names of lawyers, doctors, financial planners, religious or spiritual leader, banks and brokers, as well as locations of important papers and initial steps that should be taken once you are either gone or mentally incapacitated. It should also contain the policy numbers for your life insurance policies as well as your beneficiaries and the dollar amounts to be distributed. For anything you have stored on a computer, make sure that it will be available to your estate.

My father had his first heart attack when he was 62. I went out to Philadelphia to the hospital where he was admitted as he was about to go in for an angioplasty. He reached over and told me that he had a copy of his will and a list of non-cash assets with special instructions at home on his PC. He wanted me to go home and review the documents in case I had any questions. Well, I ran home and found his PC, which is when the first problem arose, because I didn't know his password and so I could not log in. I laughed and called him for it. The whole time, my mother was going nuts because I was bothering by dad with this trivial request and causing undo stress to the situation not realizing that my father had asked me to do it. Dad gave me his password, and I was able to log in and then access the "Will Maker Package" that he told me had used. Again, a password was required that I did not have. I thought it ironic that my father had gone to all the effort and trouble to make sure that his affairs were in order so it would be easier on his wife and kids to comply with his wishes, and that it could all be for naught because we could not access it. So, make sure that you have provided passwords and instructions to someone you trust, or make sure you leave the information in a place where it can be found and accessed. It may be best if the family attorney has an archived copy. Also, leave a copy with your spouse, significant other or best friend, if necessary. It should contain your social security number or card, as well as your passport and a copy of your birth certificate. You may also want to include a copy of your last tax return, as well as your tax accountant's name and contact information. If you have any online accounts, make sure that you leave your passwords and web addresses for all of your accounts. I would also suggest leaving a list of your assets and a list of assets that expire upon your death and any options there may be to convert those assets to alternative owners though a donor program or the like. Also, make sure that your entire vehicle inventory is available, and that you have left the titles or lease documents and vehicle registration information in an easily accessible place. It would also be convenient to your heirs if you left letters authorizing the use of the cars for anyone that is helping with your estate cleanup so in case they get a ticket, the police have the documentation they may need to prove the car has not been stolen, and that they are authorized as agents of your estate to be using it.

OREGON FORMS

The Oregon Form is used to communicate to your care providers the information they will need to make you comfortable when something goes wrong. I would suggest that you print one of the forms found in the back of the book and fill it out and distribute it to your care providers.

I would suggest that you submit the form to any facility that you have the possibility of using between now and later. Make sure that your spouse, caretakers, trustee for the trust and your attorney all have a copy of it, and that it is kept up to date. Your caregivers will depend on it being correct and will probably administer medications according to it.

CREATING A DISTRACTION

I have found that the more things that I can do that are not focused on this disease, the easier it is to maintain a positive mental attitude about life. As you can see, this is not always easy, but I believe it is critical. Whether it's spending time with your kids, gardening, playing golf, attending your grandson's sporting events, spending time with neighbors, finding religion, adopting a pet, finding a charity that can use your help or finding ways to utilize the talents that are quickly becoming dated from your old career - do something. Do not let your life become a pity party. There is too much out there for you to do! Just pick something and go do it - you have nothing to lose and everything to gain.

This is not only true for you, but chances are for your family, as well. Try not to make your situation the center of attention all the time, as I mentioned earlier on, as your situation may be more difficult to deal with for them than it is for you in some ways. Often they will need as much love and support as you do, especially when you are no longer around to support them. You may want to try to find something to do that you both like and create some memories. They will survive even after you are gone and this may provide solace in your absence.

SAYING THANK YOU

I have had the chance to say thank you throughout the story, but there are a number of people that I still owe a great debt of gratitude. These friends and family members have stepped up big time in our time of need and I only hope that I can find ways to repay their generosity and friendship. These include:

Phillip Navarre who not only helped with his expertise in legal matters but has been a pillar of strength in helping us deal with the situation created by a divorce and a remarriage situation.

Julie Navarre and Jamie Welch – Who stepped up and took on the role of editors of my rough draft and helped me, make sense out of the document. This happened despite the fact that the demands for their time came at the worse possible moment from a personal schedule standpoint.

Pat and Vince Blake as well as Don and Liz Disbrow- Our dearest neighbors in Interlochen and the rest of the Penn Loch Colony Association who were there helping us every step of the way.

My high school buddy Kim Allen (ski) and his wife Andi including their great kids Phil, Matt and Christi; for their support spiritually through friendship and helping with the moving process. As well as adopting our boat when we learned we were not going to be able to use it anymore.

Along with another high school buddy Dave Champion (Champ) and his wife Tina including their wonderful kids Brandon, Lauren and Taylor for their support in the move process as well as their part in putting together some of the fund raising events supporting our charities.

Appendix A - the checklist

An Easy Reference Guide to "Lessons Learned"

➤ **Understanding your new financial statement: Lesson Learned -** understanding the rules and making sure they work in your favor can be very valuable.

➤ **Understanding your sources of income: Lesson Learned** - regardless of how healthy you think you are, make sure you have ample financial coverage in case of a disability.

➤ **Long-term disability: Lesson Learned –** double check the contribution percentage that your company reports to the LTD insurance carrier and eventually to the IRS.

➤ **Long-term care benefits: Lesson Learned –** The EMC Human Resources group has been invaluable to me during this process. I will continue to trust and confide in them, because their assistance has greatly aided me in being able to present to you a very positive financial outcome, instead of how to effectively fight off bankruptcy and avoid creditors. I will continue to double check every piece of advice and information given to me to make sure of its accuracy and pertinence to my situation.

➤ **Overview of the situation: Lesson Learned:** All the websites you may research contain very scientific information and can be very confusing if you know nothing of the disease. This, combined with an alphabet soup list of acronyms, has the potential of confusing your loved ones and friends as you attempt to explain your diagnosis, especially if you have a Young Onset situation.

➤ **Overview of the situation: Lesson Learned** – First, make it a priority to share the news with your loved ones in person. If that is not possible, I would suggest that you put something in writing and send it to them so they have some notes to reinforce their memory, and when they talk to other family members, they can speak to the facts of your situation and not averages based on a population group that may be quite older than you. Secondly, look for a web site that best fits your needs for this situation and direct them to this site for further information. There are many sites out there, including our own.

➤ **TriMix: Lesson Learned - #1** - Your Doctor will give you a range of how much your injection should be. They will tell you to gradually increase your dosage until you are comfortable with the results. Take conservative steps as you try the different levels. Too big a jump may lead to a four-hour plus erection and a trip to the doctor's office. Just think of the ED commercials and their statement that an erection lasting more than 4 hours may be a rare, but serious, side effect. It may sound like a good idea to stretch it out to a four-hour love making session, but you may want to consider your current medical situation and whether you or your partner are up to it physically. Otherwise, the risk reward factor may not be as good as you think.

➤ **TriMix: Lesson Learned - #2 -** You and your partner need to talk about the use of this drug prior to the time you plan

142

on using it. It can be an awkward situation pulling out a vile and needle in bed or in the bathroom just prior to making love. Depending on your and your partner's maturity level regarding sexual subjects, you may want to get her involved in the application process, especially if you have a serious tremor. It is very difficult to get the needle to the right place if you are experiencing coordination problems. If you miss, it doesn't work, and you have only added to your frustration.

➢ **Trip to Cancun: Lesson Learned** - We give Hilton Gardens our Handicap Hotel Award - in particular, the franchise in O'Fallon, Missouri. On the other side of the coin, we give the Hilton Hotel in Cancun, Mexico our Rubber Chicken Award for the hotel that least lived up to our expectations. This is for multiple reasons. The rooms that were billed as handicap accessible were not by most definitions. I will give them a point for having rails behind the toilets, but 20 points off for not having rails on either side of the toilet that you could use to stand up with and 10 points off for not having toilets of proper height. The shower also gets 20 points off for lack of handles and no detachable wand. The bellman staff gets full credit for having sufficient wheelchairs and getting us to the room.

➢ **Honest officer, I'm not drunk and I wasn't driving: Lesson Learned #1** - Make sure that you understand the Hotel definition of a handicap accessible room and that it accommodates your situation.

➢ **Honest officer, I'm not drunk and I wasn't driving: Lesson Learned #2** - For International flights do not be shy in asking for wheelchair assistance in the big airports. It is too far to walk and too many lengthy lines in dealing with customs and immigration. The wheelchair assistant knows all of the shortcuts and can easily cut a half hour off your trip. Tip them well. If you don't get a wheelchair at the gate, you will have a hard time securing one, so don't leave the gate area without one.

➢ **Honest officer, I'm not drunk and I wasn't driving: Lesson Learned #3 -** Human Nature will always find its way into the equation if you appear different then everyone else. Someone will always assume the worst of your behavior. Educate those around you about your condition, as it may save some aggravation for you and others in potential situations.

➢ **Your care facility: Lesson Learned** – When seeking a nurse or caregiver, seek a match based on both technical capabilities as well a how flexible they are about what they are willing to do. If things continue the way they are, we may need the person to help edit newsletters or books or to pitch in on one of the projects we have in development. With me running the ideas by both a new person and Melanie, who knows how this could work out. What I need now is to find ways to monetize some of the pilot activities I have started. There is no one out there more anxious then me to be able to return my social security check for a while. If the project that we are proposing to the President as I write this chapter comes to fruition, there should be enough work and budget to hire an aide that is capable of helping out on some other fronts as well. We have also talked about better leveraging our support groups' talents in both St. Louis and Traverse City. There is a lot of talent there currently sitting idle. By combining efforts, we could be reducing our daily living expenses and working toward the goals of the project. This would make a good rehabilitation project to get some of these guys back into the workforce and offer a valuable support service over the phone or internet. I know the individuals involved with the Traverse City YOPD Group and I will be contacting the group in St. Charles, Missouri shortly to find out their interest in any kind of projects.

> **Your Human Resources Group: Lesson Learned -** If I would have gotten a hold of Jack or some of the senior members of his staff a little sooner, I may have been able to better utilize some of the things they have been working on with WebMD at least in a beta mode.

> **Get your act together: Lesson Learned -** People are usually very understanding and even compassionate when they understand your dilemma. Get the word out as soon as possible, and you will improve everyone's experience. Once I get this book finished, I intend to carry around a signed copy that I can hand to people when their curiosity results in a conversation. You would be surprised how many people I strike up a conversation with who tell me they have a friend or loved one that they have been curious about for years, but they have either been afraid to ask, or the person was unwilling to share.

> **Focus on what is important: Lesson Learned -** Sometimes you have to go one for one to be successful instead of four for ten. You just need to figure out when.

> **Dystonia**: A neurologic movement disorder characterized by sustained muscle contractions, resulting in repetitive, involuntary, twisting or writhing movements and unusual postures or positioning. Dystonia may be limited to specific muscle groups (focal dystonia), such as dystonia affecting muscles of the neck (cervical dystonia or spasmodic torticollis) or the eyes, resulting in closure of the eyelids (blepharospasm). Dystonia is associated with certain underlying genetic disorders, such as dystonia musculorum deformans, dopa-responsive dystonia, and paroxysmal kinesigenic and paroxysmal non-kinesigenic dystonic choreoathetosis. The condition may result from the use of certain medications, lack of oxygen during or immediately after birth, or other causes of brain trauma.

> **Dopamine**: Dopamine is a chemical that is known as a neurotransmitter. Neurotransmitters help relay messages from one nerve cell to another. Dopamine is especially important in relaying messages about movement.

> **Parkinsonism**: A constellation of the following symptoms: tremor, rigidity, bradykinesia (slow movements), and loss of postural reflexes. Although classically seen in Parkinson disease, parkinsonism may have other causes. In the elderly, parkinsonism may be caused by dopamine-blocking drugs,

multiple system atrophy, striatonigral degeneration, Shy-Drager syndrome, corticobasal degeneration, diffuse Lewy body disease, and Alzheimes disease with parkinsonism. In younger people, parkinsonism may be caused by juvenile-onset dystonia or parkinsonism, Westphal variant of Huntington disease, Wilson disease, L-dopa-responsive dystonia, Hallervorden-Spatz disease, and progressive pallidal degeneration

2068513

Made in the USA